Reminiscences of Daniel O'Connell

CLASSICS OF IRISH HISTORY
General Editor: Tom Garvin

Original publication dates of reprinted titles are given in brackets

Reminiscences of Daniel O'Connell

During the Agitations of the Veto, Emancipation and Repeal

✳

WILLIAM COOKE TAYLOR

edited by Patrick Maume

UNIVERSITY COLLEGE DUBLIN PRESS
Preas Choláiste Ollscoile Bhaile Átha Cliath

First published by Fisher, Son, & Co. London and
Cumming & Ferguson, Dublin, 1847

This edition first published by
University College Dublin Press 2005

Introduction and notes © Patrick Maume 2005

ISBN 1-904558-25-9
ISSN 1393-6883

University College Dublin Press
Newman House, 86 St Stephen's Green
Dublin 2, Ireland
www.ucdpress.ie

Cataloguing in Publication data available from the British Library

Typeset in Ireland in Ehrhardt by Elaine Shiels, Bantry, Co. Cork
Text design by Lyn Davies, Frome, Somerset, England
Printed on acid-free paper in Ireland by ColourBooks, Dublin

CONTENTS

Note on the text

The text has been re-set from the original 1847 edition. Taylor's authorship is stated in his *Daily News* obituary and confirmed by the recycled material from his journalism which appears in it.

INTRODUCTION

Patrick Maume

William Cooke Taylor was born in Youghal, County Cork on 16 April 1800. His father, Richard Taylor, was a manufacturer; resentment at the way in which a self-perpetuating clique allied to a powerful local landlord controlled the town's corporation helped to shape his son's beliefs.[2] Taylor absorbed local traditions of the horrors of repression in 1798, when suspected rebels were hanged from the Tower House and many locals were flogged and transported.[3] (He later edited a London reprint of the memoirs of the United Irishman William Sampson,[4] and wrote the general historical introduction for R. R. Madden's *The United Irishmen: Their Lives and Times*.[5]) These memories influenced Taylor's abiding view of the Irish parliament as a tyrannical and corrupt landlord assembly; from his earliest Irish magnum opus, *History of the Civil Wars in Ireland*, he declared that the Union had been a necessary precondition of Irish reform, and that Catholic Emancipation and parliamentary reform, coupled with growing British awareness of Ireland's economic potential, would lead to full integration of Ireland within the United Kingdom.[6]

On both sides of his family Taylor was descended from Cromwellian settlers; his mother, Mary Cooke, had the regicide John Cooke as ancestor. (Taylor claims he was still remembered locally as a just judge.)[7] Taylor's near-contemporary, the antiquarian Rev. Samuel Hayman (1818–86) describes a contemporary who as a child was warned by his grandfather never to trust Papists, reinforced by a description of how he had heard from his own grandfather of the family's sufferings when imprisoned during the Jacobite wars.[8] The siege mentality of this inbred Protestant community was epitomised for Taylor by a dispute at the parish church in 1810, when it was discovered that a new plasterwork design incorporated two crosses. 'Had the Pope come in person to celebrate high mass in the church, greater indignation could not have been displayed by the pious Protestants of Youghal. They averred . . . that the image of Baal had been erected in the sanctuary . . . There were a few who defended the crosses, and they were at once set down as Papists. Some others laughed at the whole proceedings, and were of course stigmatized as infidels.' The crosses were gouged out to be replaced by two crudely modelled bibles; when Taylor subsequently moved to England, he was surprised to see that the Church of England routinely placed crosses on its church buildings.[9] Agrarian violence was endemic in the countryside; in his edition of Gustave de Beaumont's book on Ireland Taylor recalls how as a boy he once took down a notice posted on a gate to see what it said. It was a Ribbon warning notice; he was promptly seized by several men standing nearby, who only released him after he had satisfied them that he acted from curiosity rather than hostility.[10]

After education at a local school Taylor entered Trinity College on 13 January 1817. He withdrew in 1820; after unsuccessfully competing for a scholarship in 1821 he returned to Youghal, when he may have witnessed the effects of the 1822 famine, as assistant-master of his old school. He then returned to Trinity and graduated BA in 1825, winning prizes in Hebrew and in English poetry and prose composition. Despite Trinity's Toryism, Taylor was always proud of the university, which recognised him as a distinguished graduate; in 1835 it granted him a LLD *honoris causa*, and his Whiggery did not exclude him from contributing to the *Dublin University Magazine*. (In 1842 he contrasted the situation in his student days, when 'a book published in Ireland had just as little chance of becoming known in London as if it had made its first appearance in Melville Island or Kamtschatka' with the contemporary situation where 'Irish talent finds a market in its own country, and, no matter what may be their politics, every Irishman ought to feel proud of two such periodicals as the *Dublin University Magazine* and the *Citizen*.')[11]

Taylor returned again to Youghal as a schoolmaster and produced school editions of grammars, catechisms and histories before emigrating to London in 1829. He rapidly became a Whig-radical publicist and a leading contributor to various journals (notably the weekly *Athenaeum*, whose policy of anonymity for contributors has helped to obscure Taylor's significance as a commentator on Irish affairs). He wrote extensively on Irish matters, on political economy, on history, on comparative religion, and on travellers' accounts of the Empire. Many of Taylor's Trinity contemporaries ended up in India as soldiers and officials; Taylor viewed the imperial mission as the dissemination of reason, religion and improvement in much the same spirit advanced by Macaulay's Minute on Indian Education. Taylor was also a founder member of the British Association and sat on its Statistical Information Committee. In 1836 Taylor revisited Youghal to marry his cousin Marianne Taylor; they had three surviving children, and at least one more died in infancy.

Taylor prided himself on his classical and Hebrew learning, and it seems likely that he was originally intended for the Church. He maintained a strong interest in religious affairs, and was decisively influenced by the latitudinarianism of Richard Whately. Taylor adopted Whately's view that Christianity was eminently ethical, rational, and law-governed; divisions within Christianity derived from misreadings of the biblical texts by commentators who mistook metaphors for literal assertions, and the national church should downplay insistence on doctrinal uniformity in order to create an all-embracing Christian body, acting in conjunction with the state to instil the moral and intellectual truths necessary for the advancement of civilisation. The members of such a church might disagree on inessentials, but were united on the essential truths of rational Christianity.[12] (Whately's critics, such as John Henry Newman, argued that dogma – and hence disagreement – was intrinsic to faith, and that Whately's principles might be extended beyond their author's intentions to deny supernaturalism altogether.)

Taylor believed a modus vivendi could be reached with Rome on a Whatelyan basis. He disliked both Calvin and Luther, and attributed the Reformation to a misunderstanding – 'Had a Ganganelli occupied the throne of St. Peter instead of a Caraffa, England would have not have been lost to the Holy See, the ascetic Reformers would have become founders of new monastic orders, and the Council of Trent, instead of accumulating the scholastic follies of former ages into a creed of interminable length, would have adopted a simple and general formula, which might have been acceptable to all the churches of Christendom'.[13] In the 1830s Taylor became a friend of Whately and worked with him in defending the National School system against Catholic and Church of Ireland supporters of denominational education. (Taylor also collaborated with Whately's ally and former secretary Charles Dickinson, Bishop of Meath, on a book advising bishops how to carry out their episcopal office.)[14] Taylor advocated a nondenominational (though specifically Christian) British education system based on the Irish model, and in the 1840s proposed that the Queen's Colleges should operate on the same principles. He suggested Whately's *Evidences of Christianity* as compulsory reading for all students, with separate divinity professors and catechists to instruct them in the particular tenets of their faiths.[15]

As a rationalist and reformer Taylor maintained a lively interest in the many varieties of human unreason and a desire to debunk them. He wrote extensively on the history of false prophets and occult beliefs (sometimes with local references; his account of John Dee compares the Elizabethan alchemist's belief that it was possible to communicate with spirits by gazing into a polished black stone with the local belief that it was possible to foretell the future by gazing into the pool of the waterfall at Glandine, near Youghal).[16] His *History of the Civil Wars in Ireland* (1831) resembles a black comedy in its account of the horrors and follies of Irish history. His descriptions of Elizabethan massacres and the use of torture to extort evidence against inconvenient landowners during the Plantations incorporate reminders that readers who doubt such horrors really occurred should study the events of 1798;[17] the downfall of the sixteenth-century viceroy Sir John Perrot is implicitly compared to the 1795 overthrow of the pro-Emancipation Lord Fitzwilliam by the Dublin Castle 'cabal',[18] a sixteenth-century rising inspired by a false prophecy is compared to the effect of the millennial 'Pastorini' prophecies on the Munster Rockites in the 1820s,[19] and Taylor's account of the seventeenth-century Remonstrant controversy in the Irish Catholic community (between supporters and opponents of the Pope's temporal authority) recalls the Veto controversy – including the wry reflection that Protestant support for the Remonstrant cause had the unfortunate though understandable effect of making many Catholics suspicious of it.[20] (Daniel O'Connell, in his *Memoir of Ireland: Native and Saxon* and his 1841 Belfast speech, cited the book as a Protestant historian's recognition of the unmerited sufferings of Irish Catholics,[21] while Henry Cooke denounced Taylor as a liar equal in mendacity to O'Connell.[22]) He used his extensive knowledge of biblical history and languages to poke fun at wild interpretations of the sacred text produced by the 'mystic school' of ultra-Evangelicals.[23]

The downside of this approach was intellectual arrogance; a self-image as a detached observer in the human zoo. The belief that one has a monopoly on reason leads easily to the assumption that anyone who thinks differently is dishonest or insane; Taylor's desire to debunk ended by trivialising history as a record of the follies and foibles of the great who had not received the advantages of nineteenth-century civilisation, and by a readiness to assume that foolish or unpleasant actions resulted from personal pique or minor disputes. It is characteristic of Taylor's self-certainty that he did not merely disagree with Ignatius Loyola's image of the world as a battleground fought over by the armies of Jesus and Satan; he found it completely unintelligible and did not see how anyone in their right mind could hold such a view.[24] Taylor fully shared Whately's view that popular education (especially in political economy) would lead the lower orders to realise that their best interests lay in accepting the leadership of their (suitably enlightened) superiors. He was entirely opposed to trade unions, which he equated with the agrarian secret societies of rural Ireland.[25]

Taylor's anti-aristocratic views, and his belief that laissez-faire was divinely ordained to sweep away the suffocating network of *ancien régime* vested interests and unleash the forces of production to the benefit of all, aligned him with the Anti-Corn Law League. In 1842 he published *A Tour of the Manufacturing Districts of Lancashire*, dedicated to Whately; this work, which provides a valuable eye-witness account of Lancashire during the Industrial Revolution, defends the manufacturing system against its critics and argues that abolition of the Corn Laws is the providentially ordained solution to trade depression and Chartism.[26] The book, presented as the work of an independent expert, was secretly commissioned by the Anti-Corn Law League (though fully consistent with views which Taylor expressed elsewhere). Taylor's magnum opus, *The Natural History of Civilisation* (1840), inspired by Whately, sees the rise and fall of Rome and Carthage as conditioned by struggle between plebeian free traders and patrician restrictionists, while presenting English history since 1066 as a Saxon struggle against Norman feudal constraints on productive commerce; Norman McCord calls Taylor the League's 'tame historian'.[27] Taylor's experience of Irish ethnic and sectarian divisions predisposed him towards the 'Norman Yoke' theory; he argued that ever since the Norman Conquest England had witnessed a struggle between the Norman aristocracy and the oppressed Saxons who comprised not merely the peasantry but also the urban commercial classes.[28] In his review of O'Connell's *Memoir of Ireland, Native and Saxon*, Taylor argues that the Saxons had nothing to do with the conquest of Ireland; they suffered as much as the Irish under the feudal yoke.[29] From 1843 until the repeal of the Corn Laws in 1846, Taylor edited the League's London-based journal, *The League*. (His collaborators included the working-class journalist Alexander Somerville, who reported on rural conditions, signing himself 'The Whistler After the Plough'.)[30]

In the early 1840s Taylor established contact with Thomas Davis; they shared a similar background as small-town Protestant professionals from the Blackwater Valley, seeking to articulate a political vision which would reconcile the inbred Protestant bigotry of the towns and the untutored Catholic violence of the countryside. Taylor helped to secure Young Ireland support for the Queen's Colleges and tried to persuade Davis to accept the Union.[31] Their common aims were epitomised by their attendance at the 1843 British Association conference in Cork. Taylor organised a public meeting in Youghal addressed by some of the conference delegates, followed by a tour of the Blackwater as far north as Fermoy; the Catholic antiquarian J. R. O'Flanagan (whose conference paper on the Blackwater was subsequently published with Taylor's assistance) recalled with pride how Catholic and Protestant clergy joined at Youghal to discuss the economic development of Ireland.[32]

After repeal of the Corn Laws in 1846, the leading Free Trader C. P. Villiers recommended Taylor's services to the principal patron of his last years – Villiers's brother George, fifth Earl of Clarendon. In 1847, just after completing the *Reminiscences of O'Connell*, Taylor returned to Ireland. Clarendon, now Lord-Lieutenant, faced a famine-stricken Ireland where most Irish newspapers and politicians, from the Young Irelanders of the *Nation* to the Orange Tories of the *Evening Mail*, were united in denouncing the Government. After commissioning Taylor to write a pamphlet defending the National Schools against Church of Ireland critics,[33] the Lord-Lieutenant decided Taylor's wide knowledge and facile pen made him uniquely well-suited to educate the Irish reading public in the merits of the Government's case, while his personal prestige would attract young intellectuals away from disaffection to the safer shores of Whiggery.[34] Clarendon persuaded Lord John Russell to appoint Taylor as Government statistician, with the promise of a permanent position if one fell vacant while the Whigs were still in office.[35] (Taylor was considered as a possible first president for Queen's College Cork, but lost out to the scientist Sir Robert Kane.) Taylor became one of the founders of the Statistical and Social Inquiry Society of Ireland, which had Whately as its first president and attempted to carry out Whately's project of educating the population of Ireland in Political Economy.[36] At the same time, Taylor wrote much of the anonymous editorial content in Frederick William Conway's *Dublin Evening Post*, the only reputable pro-Government Dublin paper; the *Post* argued that the Government was doing its best and that much of the misery suffered by the poor was due to landlords who evicted their tenants rather than live up to their obligations. When the European revolutions of 1848 made the Young Ireland movement into a serious insurrectionary threat, Taylor turned his fire on them; Clarendon believed Taylor's *Evening Post* articles predicting a massacre of Catholic clergy by 'Irish Jacobins' were decisive in alienating clerical opinion from the Young Irelanders.[37]

Taylor welcomed distinguished visitors to Dublin. On 29 August 1849 he discussed Irish history with Macaulay; the historian (whose style and worldview resembled Taylor's own) was impressed by his 'character and talents'.[38] Thomas Carlyle was less impressed when he dined with Taylor at a friend's house on 4 July 1849, acidly describing his 'lazy, gurgling, semi-masticated, semi-deceitful (and self-deceiving) speech, thought and action . . . gurgle-snuffle, Cockney-and-Youghal wit . . . and now . . . I learn that he is dead of cholera . . . and the curtains rush down between us impenetrable for evermore. Allah akbar, Allah Kerim!'[39]

Taylor died in Dublin on 12 September 1849. His literary admirers of all parties petitioned successfully for his widow to be granted a pension; in accordance with the tenets of political economy, they noted that the plight of Taylor's family did not derive from improvidence but from his sudden and unforeseeable death.[40]

Taylor's descendants remained active in Liberal politics; his Glasgow-based son, Richard Whately Cooke Taylor, wrote for the *Athenaeum* advocating Irish land reform on the principles of John Stuart Mill. A grandson, C. R. Cooke Taylor, was secretary of the Irish Literary Society; he was briefly interned in Bulgaria during the First World War.[41] The last member of the Taylor family to live in Youghal was Susan Taylor, who died in the 1890s.[42]

REMINISCENCES OF DANIEL O'CONNELL

The *Reminiscences of Daniel O'Connell* reflects the ethos of the *Athenaeum* and other early nineteenth-century reviews, which imposed anonymity on individual contributors and fostered a collective 'voice' of the journal – brash, argumentative, ideologically committed, often witty. Taylor's account of O'Connell combines some of his own memories with material drawn from his numerous *Athenaeum* reviews of books on Ireland.[43] Some eye-witness material is clearly identifiable. Taylor's description of O'Connell walking to the Four Courts followed by a crowd of admirers is used by Oliver MacDonagh, who cites the book as the work of 'an acute contemporary ... by no means an uncritical admirer of O'Connell'.[44] The 'Munster Farmer's' claims to have personally witnessed the 1818 attack on Grattan by an anti-vetoist mob and to have seen a Catholic funeral in a Protestant graveyard forcibly dispersed by order of the Evangelical Archbishop Magee may also be taken at face value. (Taylor loved to mock the incongruous sight of Irish ultra-Protestants professing to uphold Christianity by denouncing the Cross and the Virgin Mary as 'Popish'; here he enquires why Biblical texts incorporated in the Catholic funeral service should become blasphemous idolatries when pronounced in Latin rather than English.) The account of Sheil's speech on the defeat of the 1826 Catholic Relief Bill also appears to be drawn from life. Taylor may also draw on the memories of his ally, the Irish Whig editor, Frederick William Conway; their interpretations of O'Connell's career coincide on many points.

Essentially, this book is high-class journalism; a first draft of history by an intelligent Irish Whig, whose perspective on Daniel O'Connell is important for its view of the Liberator and the insights it provides into the worldview of O'Connell's ambivalent Whig allies.

Taylor's description of the O'Connells' smuggling activities is less hostile than it might appear at first sight (though the reference to wrecking, with the comment that the O'Connells never practised it, might argue otherwise). As a Free Trader Taylor thought smuggling a natural response to the idiocy of tariff barriers. Elsewhere he presents the eighteenth-century illicit wine trade between France and Munster as proof that commerce overcomes religious and ethnic divisions:

> A double colonisation of exiles supported this trade. Exiled Irish Catholics settled in France – and a great number of Huguenot families driven from their homes by the *Dragonades* established themselves in Ireland. It may be added, that both suffered persecution without learning mercy. The Irish were active in the warfare against the Protestants of the Cevennes; and there were no more ardent supporters of the Penal Code than the descendants of the French Refugees. Claret, however, produced personal relations between those who were politically opposed; and we have heard many a tradition of a Huguenot saved by a wine-grower at the request of an Irish importer, and of a Catholic protected by a wine-merchant to gratify a French exporter.[45]

On the other hand, Taylor's account of the ascetic fervour of O'Connell's later years reflects the fact that as a believer in a political economy founded on hedonism, Taylor disapproved of asceticism on principle. Reading back the fervent piety of O'Connell's later life into his earlier career, Taylor assumes he was permanently shaped by his education at St Omer. Taylor is unaware that between 1795 and 1808 O'Connell lapsed from Catholicism and adhered to Deism (this only became generally known with the publication of his 1795–1802 journal in 1905).[46] This misapprehension was encouraged by Taylor's reliance on the pious John O'Connell's account of his father's life and speeches, from which the account of O'Connell's work practices is drawn.

The core of Taylor's account lies in his description of the Veto controversy and the Emancipation campaign. This reflects Taylor's ambivalence about popular agitation (presented simultaneously as uplifting an oppressed people and as irresponsibly evoking forces beyond the leaders' control) and about O'Connell's verbal vitriol, an attack on deference which could be seen both as courageous defiance of oppression and as poisoning the wells of public discourse.[47] The Catholic Association was both an obvious model for the Anti-Corn Law League and an affront to Whig elitism suspiciously resembling the detested Chartists. As an Erastian who believes the Church should function as a virtual department of state and sees Whig official patronage as an honourable reward for public service rather than an instrument of corruption, Taylor cannot see why Catholics should fear state influence over their clergy. (He quite reasonably points out that non-Catholic monarchs elsewhere in Europe exercised similar privileges; less reasonably, he suggests the veto could not have been used to any great extent, without noting that even under these conditions it could have exercised a 'chill factor' on clerical attitudes.) Taylor presents O'Connell's resistance to state influence over the clergy in purely religious rather than political terms – a simple attempt, motivated by religious zeal, to extend the power of the priests, rather than an attempt to co-opt the priests for O'Connell's own political project. (The two are not mutually exclusive; Taylor's interpretation of the early O'Connell is coloured by the memory of the pietistic opponent of the Queen's Colleges – whose opposition reflected suspicion of government jobbery as well as fear of religious indifferentism.)

Taylor's argument that by refusing to compromise on the Veto O'Connell retarded Emancipation as much as his subsequent actions advanced it incidentally gives a striking description of how Moore's *Irish Melodies* influenced elite support for Catholic Emancipation. While Taylor shows the opponents of Emancipation strengthened O'Connell by driving the Catholics into his hands, he downplays, without entirely denying, the extent to which their 'obstinacy and bigotry' enjoyed widespread popular support in Britain. At one point he suggests that O'Connell mistakenly attributed the hostility of Prime Ministers Addington and Liverpool to the British people as a whole; elsewhere he admits the existence of widespread popular bigotry but suggests it is being eroded by the march of intellect.

Taylor agrees with O'Connell's nationalist critics in seeing the campaign for Catholic Emancipation as his great achievement and the years after 1829 as an anticlimax; but where nationalist critics attributed O'Connell's failure to his temporising with the Whigs and unwillingness to campaign unremittingly for Repeal by every means necessary, Taylor regrets that he did not abandon Repeal and unequivocally embrace Whiggery. O'Connell's refusal to accept the Union is attributed to a combination of personal conservatism and pique at his humiliation in the House of Commons debate on the Doneraile Conspiracy. (Most commentators see O'Connell as a more successful Parliamentary figure than Taylor suggests. He was a good set-piece speaker though less suited to the cut and thrust of debate.)

Insofar as Taylor allows any rationality to the Repeal agitation, he ascribes it to resentment of 'that spirit of commercial monopoly which has too often been a guiding motive in the policy of England'. (Hence, he implies, the repeal of the Corn Laws will cement the Union.) O'Connell is blamed for the violence of the Tithe War of the early 1830s (when describing similar agrarian violence in the 1820s, Taylor places the blame exclusively on the opponents of reform).

Although Taylor acknowledges Earl Grey's hostility to O'Connell as excessive, the Whigs are given full credit for the Irish reforms of the late 1830s, with O'Connell reduced to a troublesome suppliant for patronage. The limitations of these reforms are attributed exclusively to irresponsible Tory opposition, without acknowledging Whig reluctance. (How far would the Whigs have made concessions if they had not been politically dependent on O'Connell?)

Taylor emphasises O'Connell's early conservatism and opportunistic attempts at rapprochement with Orangeism in the early 1830s to suggest O'Connell was a Tory at heart. (This reflects the fact that after 1829 O'Connell was often more hostile to Irish Liberal Unionists who refused to accept his leadership than to Tories, whom he regarded as straightforward enemies.) O'Connell's oft-repeated hyperbole that he would be prepared to accept the re-enactment of the entire Penal Code if necessary to regain the Irish Parliament is taken at face value (understandably, since Taylor emphasises how far the Irish Parliament was implicated in the bloody repressions of the 1790s and the role of Orange ultras in opposing the Act of Union).

Taylor ignores O'Connell's consistent commitment to such reformist causes such as Jewish Emancipation and the abolition of slavery. (Taylor's journalism voices contemporary liberal criticisms of O'Connell's ambivalence towards Spanish and French Liberalism;[48] in view of the links between early nineteenth-century European Catholicism and political absolutism, most later commentators are impressed that O'Connell supported continental liberalism in any form.) There is one exception. Taylor emphasises O'Connell's consistent opposition to the Corn Laws, ignoring the tensions in his relationship with the Anti-Corn Law League.[49] O'Connell's speech to a League meeting in Covent Garden Theatre, London in February 1844 while awaiting sentence after conviction on dubious charges of 'unlawful and seditious opposition' was the most notable of the periodical political spectacles which the League presented at this venue. The crowd displayed enthusiasm for O'Connell as a victim of legal persecution which might yet be deployed against themselves; O'Connell responded warmly, while

Taylor and Somerville wrote up the occasion in the League's paper.[50] Taylor presents this in retrospect as the symbolic reconciliation of O'Connell with the British people, after which Repeal was essentially abandoned. O'Connell's struggle against the Young Irelanders is presented as vital in preventing an armed revolt, and Taylor suggests that if there had been a conflict the old man would have fought for the Union. His failure to embrace the Union in word as well as deed is attributed to desire to retain popularity with a populace corrupted by his long career of irresponsible rhetoric.

For Taylor O'Connell is a transitional figure, scarred by per-secution in youth, by an archaic Catholic education, and by the adulation of an oppressed people who looked to him for a leadership to which he was, with all his abilities, unequal. With the implemen-tation of political and economic reform and the spread of universal education, the conditions which produced him will disappear and Ireland will settle down within the Union. Like Clarendon,[51] Taylor saw the Repeal movement as a transitional phenomenon whose disintegration would clear the way for Ireland's regeneration.

Taylor's last phase as spin-doctor for Whig famine policy colours his historical reputation ever since. Gavan Duffy writes scornfully of how 'Dr Cooke Taylor . . . undertook to demonstrate the absurdity of his native country expecting the control of her own affairs'.[52] Christine Kinealy notes the financial rewards he received from Clarendon.[53] These criticisms overlook Taylor's longstanding and outspoken commitment to Irish reform; Clarendon emphasised that Taylor's salary was partly intended as compensation for liter-ary and journalistic work which he sacrificed by leaving London, and that his chances of a permanent post were uncertain.[54] Taylor was not a pure mercenary like the scandal-sheet editor James Birch (also hired by Clarendon) but an ideologue in the service of a cause which he had consistently upheld. His central failure lay elsewhere, in the doctrinaire rigidity with which he maintained a Utopian view of the prospects for transforming the Irish economy and dismissed with self-assured flippancy the cries of those who called for the government to do more for the poor.

In some respects Taylor's worldview resembles that of the great late-Victorian Irish Whig historian W. E. H. Lecky, who shared his Whatelyan latitudinarianism and belief in political economy, and who studied mediaeval European morals and the insanity of the witch-hunt for clues to the development of civilisation;[55] but where Lecky gazes back anxiously to discover what in the past has led to a present where property is threatened by 'demagogues' and a Broad Church Anglicanism diluted to the verge of agnosticism trembles before Ultramontane and Evangelical populism, Taylor's Whiggery is confident of its ability to remake the world in its own image. He looked forward to an Ireland where the National schools had trained the population in Whatelyan latitudinarian tolerance, deference and industry, an Ireland ruled on Whig principles by a gentry educated to live up to their responsibilities, where political economy would bring about the sort of transformation he had witnessed in Lancashire – or, on a smaller scale, in the new Waterford industrial village of Portlaw.[56] Instead, Taylor's account of O'Connell stands as a monument to mutual misunderstanding, a reminder of the abiding tensions which strained nineteenth-century alliances between Irish Catholic/nationalists and British and Irish Liberals, and why the ecumenical religious latitudinarianism and economic liberalism which met such widespread acceptance in late twentieth-century Ireland failed to reconcile nineteenth-century Ireland to the Union.

The two other pieces included in this volume exemplify the *Athenaeum* reviewing style, with its long quotations from the books under review. In recent years Taylor's review of Carleton's Famine novel *The Black Prophet*, with its defence of the meal-hoarder Darby Skinadre, has been recognised as a classic specimen of the doctrinaire political economist response to the Famine.[57] (Taylor's Anti-Corn Law League associate Alexander Somerville also defended Darby Skinadre.)[58] Taylor's political views did not necessarily reflect those of Youghal corn-merchants, who favoured the Corn Laws which gave them a privileged position in the British market;[59] Youghal was severely affected by Repeal, and elected the Protectionist Isaac Butt as its MP 1852–65. It is possible, however, that his denunciation of bread-riots is influenced by the widely publicised Youghal bread riots of September 1846,[60] as well as by personal memories of the 1822 famine.

The long article on 'Repeal Songs of Munster' considers O'Connellite street-ballads as a study in human folly, giving some glimpses into Catholic popular hope and resentment. Taylor was not unique in this: the administrator, Charles Edward Trevelyan, whose religious worldview resembled Taylor's, also accumulated a collection of Repeal songs.[61] It incidentally uncovers a few details of whose full significance Taylor is unaware – the original O'Connellite version of 'Come to the Bower', more familiar to later audiences in Irish-American Fenian guise; a rare example of O'Connellite millennialism associated with the 'Repeal Year' of 1843 (also, coincidentally, the year of William Miller's 'Great Disappointment') rather than the Pastorini prophecies of the 1820s; conspicuous church-building as a defiant display of growing Catholic communal confidence; the last flickers of the Munster aisling tradition, their internal rhymes carried over into English from Gaelic predecessors. Reviewing the Young Irelanders' *Spirit of the Nation* before he recognised the movement as a serious political threat in their own right, Taylor praises the melancholy strain of Davis (with whom he was not yet acquainted) and anticipates from a Unionist perspective the later Gaelic Revival complaint that Young Ireland advocacy of a distinctive Irish civilisation was undertaken in literary styles and genres derived from England. His treatment of their audience as a product of the National Schools provides a hint, which Taylor fails to grasp, that the political results of the new education system might be more complex than he anticipated.

REMINISCENCES

OF

DANIEL O'CONNELL,

ESQ., M.P.

DURING THE AGITATIONS OF

The Veto, Emancipation, and Repeal.

BY

A MUNSTER FARMER.

"Quæ ipse vidi, et quorum pars fui."—*Virgil.*
"All that I saw, and part of which I was."—*Dryden's Translation.*

FISHER, SON, & CO.
ANGEL STREET, ST. MARTIN'S-LE-GRAND, LONDON.

PREFACE

THE controversies which raged round O'CONNELL in his life-time pursue him to the tomb. It seems to be agreed, on all hands, that he was *un grand homme manqué*, but it is fiercely disputed which was his precise deficiency. A possible solution is, that there were several, and that it is an error to attribute the unquestionable barrenness of his career exclusively to one. Few who have acted with him have not also acted against him: as an ally, they appreciated his merits; as an opponent, they sought for his defects. The Munster Farmer has known him in both capacities during the greater part of his long career; and though he presumes not to pronounce judgment himself, he believes that his Reminiscences will provide valuable materials to guide the judgment of others.

Previous to 1824 O'CONNELL was unknown in England; and that mighty engine, the Catholic Association, which he so ably developed, and so efficiently worked, caused the vacillations of his early career to be forgotten in Ireland. But as the character of a powerful mind and impulsive nature is moulded, and the course of such a life predestined, by surrounding circumstances – more especially in the first stages of progress – the Munster Farmer has taken account of the sowing of the seed, the germination of the grain, the development of the plant, and the ripening of the harvest for the sickle. He was too deeply interested in the crop, to neglect watching every process of its growth. These Reminiscences might easily have been extended; but it was not the writer's purpose to make a book. O'CONNELL is said to have left behind him an autobiography, and until this is before the world, his life cannot be fairly written. Enough, however, is known, to enable us to comprehend the nature of his mission, and his adequacy to its fulfilment. These are the points to which attention is chiefly directed in the following pages. Professions of impartiality from Irishmen are not unjustly received with suspicion, and Munster Farmers are not more free from political bias than the rest of their countrymen; the writer therefore limits himself to claiming perfect accuracy in his statement of facts – many of them little known: the soundness of his opinions is a very different question, which he leaves to be solved by his readers.

Suirdale in the Glens,
June 8th, 1847.

REMINISCENCES
OF
DANIEL O'CONNELL

It has been said that the Martello Towers, like the more ancient Round Towers, were erected in Ireland for the express purpose of puzzling posterity; but Ireland has left many more difficult problems to be solved by future generations, and some of the most perplexing will probably be those connected with the political career of the remarkable man who has just departed from amongst us. DANIEL O'CONNELL, who used to boast that he was the best abused, and who might have lamented that he was the most indiscreetly praised, man in Europe, has already become the hero of more than one historical controversy; it is disputed, before the tomb has closed over his remains, whether his life was a blessing or a blunder – whether Ireland has most reason to lament his birth or his death. It is our purpose to state the facts by which this controversy ought fairly to be decided; and the strange combinations of circumstances which have raised such a controversy, not on remote and distant events, but on matters with which so many of us have been contemporary.

The family from which he sprung, the time and place of his birth, the peculiarities of his early education, and the public events which occurred in his childhood, had each and all a powerful influence in moulding his mind, and directing his future career; around his cradle were formed the passions which follow his hearse. Few personal anecdotes of his infancy and his childhood have been preserved, but all his speeches, to the very last, showed that it was a period of deep impressions and treasured recollections.

Like all the native Irish, in Kerry, the O'Connells claim descent from the Catholic royalists who shed their blood in the cause of the ungrateful Stuarts, whom Charles II allowed to be stripped of most of their property by the Act of Settlement, for loyalty to his father; and from whom William III took the remainder, for fidelity to his father-in-law. Time has now set the broad seal of prescription on the Cromwellian and Williamite settlements of Ireland; but in the last century, the descendants, or reputed descendants, of those whose estates had been forfeited, were accustomed to point out the broad lands of their ancestors to their children, and to impress upon their minds the cruelty and injustice of those by whom they had been confiscated. Like Roderick Dhu,[1] the pauperized descendant of a line of kings could point to

> Deep-waving fields and pastures green,
> With gentle groves and slopes between;

And, with more truth than the Highland chieftain, he might add,

> These fertile plains, that soften'd vale,
> Were once the birthright of the Gael;
> The stranger came with iron hand,
> And from our fathers reft the land.

Daniel O'Connell, the grandfather of the subject of the present memoir, resided at Darrynane, in the county of Kerry, where he possessed a small estate which had escaped confiscation, and held some valuable leases, which having been granted previous to the passing of the penal laws, were not subject to the enactments of that iniquitous measure. He left behind him three sons – Maurice, who inherited his lands; Morgan, who opened a kind of miscellaneous store in Cahirciveen; and Daniel, who entered into the French service. Maurice, the head of the family, was childless; but Morgan had a family of ten children, the eldest being the subject of this memoir, who was born at Carhen, near the post-town at Cahirciveen, in the county of Kerry, August 6th, 1775. The penal laws were then in full force; priest-hunting was as favourite a sport with the ultra-Protestant gentry, as fox-hunting and hare-hunting at a later period; the rituals and services of the Catholic church, proscribed by law, were celebrated in the rocky ravines and remote recesses of the mountains; any Protestant could compel his Catholic neighbour to give him up his best horse for five pounds, and this law was absolutely enforced by a Protestant squire, whose horse was worsted in a race by the steed of a Catholic gentleman. He consoled himself for his defeat, by the compulsory purchase of the winning horse. The peasants of Ireland, goaded to agrarian insurrections by intolerable oppressions, were coerced by laws, which Arthur Young declared to be 'fit only for the regions of Barbary'; and the great bulk of the Protestant clergy neglected almost every clerical duty save the levying of tithes, but in this they exhibited a zealous energy, almost amounting to severity, as if to compensate for their deficiency in everything else. But hope had already dawned for Ireland, as one of her popular prophecies predicted, in the far-distant West; the war of independence had begun in America, and, as the successes of the colonists increased, so the galling restrictions on the Irish Catholics were relaxed, partly from the necessity of conciliating them during a dangerous struggle, but chiefly from the growing liberality and intelligence of the age.

Having said so much of the time, we have next to notice some peculiarities of the place, of his birth. The rocky coast of Kerry, indented by numerous small harbours, afforded means of embarkation for the young and adventurous Irish Catholics, who, finding themselves excluded from the British army on account of their religion, sought to gratify their love of excitement by entering the Irish brigades in the service of France. 'The flights of wild geese', as the evasions of these emigrants were whimsically called, are said to have been periodical from Valentia harbour; and in consequence of this form of intercourse, what the law called smuggling, and what those engaged in it called free trade, was very active between the French ports and this part of Ireland. Morgan O'Connell's store, or shop, at Cahirciveen, received many a cargo of French laces, wines, and silks, which were sold at an immense profit in the south and west of Ireland, and enabled him rapidly to accumulate a large fortune. English cruisers avoided the iron-bound coast of Kerry, which then had a reputation even worse than its reality. It was said that the men of the Kerry coast combined wrecking with smuggling, and that for both purposes they had organised a very complete system of posts and telegraphic signals along the bluff headlands. When a suspicious sail was announced, nice calculations were made, to ascertain her probable position after nightfall; a horse was then turned out to graze on the fields near that part of the shore opposite to which she most probably was, and a lantern was tied to the horse's head. Viewed from a distance, this light, rising and falling as the animal fed, produced precisely the same effect as light in the cabin of a distant ship. The crew of the stranger-vessel, thus led to believe that there was open water before them, steered boldly onwards, and could not discover their error until they had dashed against the rocks. There is no reason to believe that the O'Connells ever engaged in such treacherous transactions; but there is indisputable evidence that they were largely practised in this part of the country, and that they offered great protection to smugglers by deterring the English cruisers from the coast.

Daniel O'Connell's infancy was thus passed amid scenes likely to impress his mind with stern hostility to the Protestant ascendancy, and the English government by which it was supported. In the name of that ascendancy, he was taught that his ancestors had been plundered; in the name of that ascendancy, he saw his religion insulted and his family oppressed, for the penal laws opposed serious impediments to his father's investment of the profits of his trade in the acquisition of land. All around him were engaged in a fiscal war with the English government, and, in the code of Kerry ethics, a seizure by the officers of the Custom House was regarded as a robbery, and the defrauding of the revenue a simple act of justice to one's self and family.

His education singularly confirmed and strengthened these feelings. At the age of thirteen he was sent with his brother Maurice to a school kept by the Rev. Mr. Harrington, a Catholic clergyman in the neighbourhood of Cork. This was the first school publicly opened and held by a Catholic priest since the penal laws; its proprietor, a gentleman of piety and learning, had suffered for his religious zeal in the past age of persecution, and he often quoted his reminiscences to illustrate the doctrines of Christian perseverance and resignation. About the year 1790, Mr. O'Connell was sent to study at the Catholic seminary of Liege, but being too old for admission, he went to Louvain, from whence he subsequently removed to St Omer and Douay. His scholastic career has been described to us as pre-eminently successful by some of his contemporaries; his diligence in study could only be equalled by his punctual attention to the ritual of his religion, and his teachers held him up as an example to his fellow-pupils both as a scholar and as a saint. Religion in O'Connell was not so much a principle, as a part of his existence; but it was the religion of an age when the Papacy and the Reformation were engaged in mortal conflict, not of a century when all except bigots saw the necessity of a treaty on the basis of *uti possidetis*, when each should rest satisfied with what it had gained, or what it still held, in Europe.

Animated by such feelings, it was impossible that the young O'Connell could view the outburst of the French Revolution with any other feelings than those of unqualified abhorrence. His uncle Daniel, whom he sincerely loved and respected, was strongly attached to the Bourbons, and was the personal friend of the king; consequently, every insult offered to royalty was a source of grief to a young man, the best sympathies of whose heart were engaged in the royalist cause. The vulgar infidelity of the French soldiers disgusted a refined intellect, and revolted a religious mind. There are fanatics of unbelief as well as of belief; such then abounded in the French army, and, on their march to the frontier through Douay, the British students there had to endure many insults and injuries from their irreligious bigotry. The difficulty of communicating with a remote part of Ireland delayed the O'Connells at Douay during part of the reign of terror; it was not until the 21ˢᵗ of December, 1793, the day of the execution of the unfortunate king, that they left Douay, and they reached Calais only just in time to embark on board the packet which brought the melancholy intelligence to England.

Among the passengers were Henry and John Sheares, two ardent young men, whose republican zeal was so violent, that they had actually bribed two national guards to lend them their uniform, that they might witness, and in some degree share in, the execution of the unhappy Louis. John is even said to have displayed as a trophy a handkerchief which he had dipped in the blood of the wretched king. O'Connell felt more than the ordinary disgust which such conduct must have produced in every honourable mind; the hatred he felt to the French republicans was directed against those who entertained similar opinions in his own country; and so strong was his anti-revolutionary feeling, that, while a law student in London, in 1794, he attended the trials of Hardy, Thelwall, and Horne Tooke, with the hope of seeing those supposed offenders against social order brought to condign punishment.[2] In 1798 Mr. O'Connell was called to the Irish bar, and began to take a part in political life. What is called the independence of the Irish parliament had at this time lasted about sixteen years, and the result of the experiment was an amount of misery, oppression, and misgovernment, which drove the great bulk of the people to desperation. The era of 1782, which O'Connell, and many of his followers, have represented as a just source of national pride and thankfulness, was really the commencement of the most corrupt and calamitous period to be found in the annals of any country. Grattan's boasted revolution established, not the independence of Ireland, but the independence of the Irish Protestant ascendancy, and compelled the English ministry to support the power, and wink at the excesses of that ascendancy, rather than peril the integrity of the empire. That ascendancy, aware that its iron rule was odious to the great mass of the population, strove to maintain its power by passing a melancholy series of statutes, not to be rivalled by the ukases of the worst of the Russian despots; they enacted, in rapid succession, a Convention act, a Riot act, an Arms' act, a Gunpowder act, an Insurrection act, an Indemnity act, a Suspension of the Habeas Corpus act, and finally, they placed the greater part of Ireland under martial law. It is utterly absurd to impute these atrocious misdeeds of the Irish parliament to the will of the English minister; it is a strange defence to make for that body, that it united excessive servility to excessive tyranny: but the excuse, such as it is, was untrue; the English ministers were deliberately deceived by the Irish ascendancy, and the tortures openly inflicted in Dublin were unblushingly denied in London.

A rebellion, to establish a republic, was planned by the United Irishmen, and was nipped in the bud. An insurrection to put an end to intolerable wrongs, was raised by the peasantry, and, after its first burst of irrepressible violence, was extinguished in blood. The two events, though nearly contemporary, were perfectly distinct; though it has served the interest of too many parties, to confound them together. It is of the greatest importance to Ireland and the empire, that the different characteristics of each should be carefully pointed out; and we shall endeavour to do so with as much brevity as the subject will allow.

The Irish rebellion of 1798 was essentially Protestant; it was planned by men, some of whom, like Lord Edward Fitzgerald, enjoyed rank and station; their minds had been inflamed by the success of the Americans in achieving independence, and by the bright promise of the early stages of the French revolution. Their great popular strength lay among the Presbyterians of the North of Ireland, lineally descended from the old Covenanters; inheritors of their principles, and, like them, intrepid assertors of freedom for themselves, without any great regard for the rights of others. The projects of the republicans were betrayed to government by a contemptible bankrupt named Thomas Reynolds, for a sum of money in hand, and a promise of future provision in another country. Reynolds had obtained a valuable lease through the influence of Lord Edward Fitzgerald, and his vehement protestations of gratitude, instead of exciting the suspicions, won the confidence of that unhappy nobleman. Government made short work with the republicans: Lord Edward Fitzgerald died of his wounds in prison; the brothers Sheares and some others were hanged; the rest made their peace with government, and after having been for some time detained in prison, contrary to the terms of the agreement, were permitted to emigrate to other lands, where most of them attained higher rank and fortune than they would probably have reached in their unhappy country. The northern republicans, though deprived of their leaders, took the field, and were irretrievably routed at the battles of Ballinahinch and Saintfield.

During all this period, O'Connell was a zealous royalist; he was a distinguished member of the yeomanry corps called the Lawyer's Artillery, and there was no more enthusiastic supporter of the government in that body.[3] In 1840 we find him denouncing the violent measures of 1798 and 1799 – 'the deprivation of all legal protection to liberty or life – the familiar use of torture – the trials by courts-martial – the forcible suppression of public meetings – the total stifling of public opinion – and the use of armed violence.' But while these deeds were being actually done, he raised not his voice against them; they certainly had his tacit sanction, and not unlikely, considering the violence of his anti-republican feelings, his warm approbation.

The insurrection of 1798 was Catholic, simply because Catholics were engaged in it; the Catholic peasants of Wexford and the mid-land counties. It was the work of a peasantry deliberately goaded to resistance by local oppression and military outrage. It was the desperate struggle of men destitute of arms, organisation, or leaders – who fought with the courage of despair, because they had no hopes of mercy. A civil war had been planned, but a Jacquerie exploded; the only connection between them being that both were the obvious and necessary result of the misrule of the Irish parliament.

A Union was necessary for the salvation of Ireland, when it became evident, to every man in his senses, that the Irish parliament was quite incapable to govern the country; an opinion which was further confirmed by its consenting to be bribed to effect its own annihilation. The Union was the vindication of the United Irishmen, and the exculpation of the misguided insurgents; it was therefore naturally opposed by O'Connell, who had been zealous against both. 'Let us', said he, 'show to Ireland that we have nothing in view but her good – nothing in our hearts but the desire of mutual forgiveness, mutual toleration, and mutual affection: in fine, *let every man who feels with me proclaim, that if the alternative were offered him of Union, or the re-enactment of the Penal Code in all its pristine horrors, that he would prefer, without hesitation, the latter, as the lesser and more sufferable evil –* that he would rather confide in the justice of his brethren, the Protestants of Ireland, who have already liberated him, than lay his country at the feet of foreigners.' 'This sentiment', says the report, 'was met with much and marked approbation'. A more unworthy sentiment was never uttered by the lips of man. The Orangemen, who then arrogated to themselves exclusively the title of 'Protestants of Ireland', would, had they not been restrained by Lord Cornwallis, have re-imposed the penal code with still more stringent and sanguinary enactments: they had nicknamed Lord Cornwallis, then lord-lieutenant, Lord Croppy-wallis, because he granted pardon to the unfortunate insurgents, whom the loyalists called 'croppies', because they did not wear pig-tails, which in those days were regarded as cognizances – more than thirty Catholic chapels had been burned, in various parts of the country – and the only complaint heard in the land was, that too much lenity had been shown in the suppression of the rebellion. The bar of Ireland was naturally opposed to the Union, which threatened to transfer a share of their business to the courts of Westminster; the shop-keepers of Dublin disliked a measure which threatened to deprive them of some portion of their trade; a large body of the Orangemen disliked it because they dreaded that the Imperial Parliament would set limits to the ascendancy which they had so grossly abused; and a more enlightened body, to which O'Connell belonged, felt proud of nationality, and not unreasonably jealous of that spirit of commercial monopoly which has too often been a guiding motive in the policy of England.

It is generally known that Pitt intended to make the Union complete, by effacing all the differences between the two nations, and admitting Catholics within the pale of the constitution. He entered into negotiations with the Catholic prelates and aristocracy, who manifested an honourable readiness to consent to any securities which might be deemed necessary to conciliate prejudice, or to draw closer the bonds of allegiance. But Pitt, who had long treated George III with rather less respect than is due from a minister to his sovereign, made no mention of his negotiations to the king; probably delaying the communication for the purpose of bringing his plans to maturity. One of his colleagues, Lord Auckland, who thought that Pitt had underrated both his talents and his services, discovered the secret, and immediately invoked the aid of the Archbishop of Canterbury to rouse the religious prejudices of the king against the proposed measure. This was no very difficult task: to opinions he had once formed, George III adhered with all the obstinacy of latent insanity; Pitt vainly endeavoured to change his mind, and, finding him inflexible, resigned. We may add, that, at the moment, Pitt was not sorry to find so plausible a pretext for evading the necessity of concluding a peace with France, which was loudly demanded by the nation.

The rebellion of Robert Emmett, if so maimed and ridiculous an insurrection deserves such a name, gave Mr O'Connell a second opportunity of appearing in the character of a flaming loyalist. It is commonly said that the English administration of the day deserved most severe censure, for not having discovered and disconcerted that insane attempt; but the fact of the case is, that the government was misled by being too well informed. Peculiar sources of information enable us to give the real history of an event which hitherto has been most grossly misrepresented.

The peace of Amiens put an end to the pretexts raised for continuing the imprisonment of the United Irishmen in Fort St George. Several of them went to France, where, soon perceiving that the peace was likely to prove nothing better than a hollow truce, they began to speculate upon the renewal of the struggle in

Ireland. Talleyrand opened a communication with them, through Dr M'Nevin; and Robert Emmett, who had only just attained the age of manhood, was admitted to an interview with Napoleon.

In 1798, Robert Emmett had been a distinguished student in Trinity College, Dublin; and he was one of those expelled by Lord Clare, when he held his memorable visitation. His elder brother, Thomas Addis Emmett, was one of the leaders of the United Irishmen, and had been one of the state prisoners. Robert had adopted the same principles, but with greater zeal and enthusiasm. He formed a plan for raising an insurrection in Ireland, simultaneous with a French invasion of England; but, with all the self-reliance of youth, he trusted more to his own inventive genius than to the promises of allies, or the advice of associates. A plot of a different nature had been previously formed by a remnant of the United Irishmen. It was connected with Colonel Despard's insane attempt of 1802, the intention being to raise an insurrection at the same time in Ireland and England. The son of an English marquis, possessing a large property in Ireland, of whose sanity some suspicions may be reasonably entertained, is said, on some authority, to have been the link of connection between the insurgents in the two islands.[4] When information of these proceedings reached the insurgents in Paris, they sent Robert Emmett home, to ascertain the state of public feeling. This he estimated more from his preconceived opinions and imagination, than from any careful inquiry. Emmett had another reason for acting alone; in the course of his brief interview, he had detected the inordinate ambition of Buonaparte, and he was resolved that Ireland should not be emancipated from England, merely to become a dependency on France. Actuated by these feelings, he broke off all communication with the parties in Paris, and, supported only by two or three as enthusiastic as himself, resolved to act quite independently. The attention of the English ministry was fixed on Paris; they had accurate information of all the transactions and discussions between the Irish refugees and the French government; they therefore knew that no recent intelligence had been received from Ireland, and they were therefore without any apprehension of danger from that quarter. The very imprudence of the leaders of the insurrection tended to disarm suspicion. On the 14th of July, they lighted bonfires to celebrate the French revolution; on the 16th, their carelessness led to an explosion and fire at their depot in Patrick-street; and the approach of an outbreak was a common topic of conversation in Dublin. In fact, Emmett's plans were so wholly his own, that the failure of his arrangements, at the critical moment of outbreak, seems to us far more likely to have been the result of defective organisation than of wilful treachery.

On the night of the 23rd of July, he set out from the place of rendezvous to storm the castle of Dublin, with not quite two hundred men, imperfectly armed, and half intoxicated. They had but a short distance to march; and, had they advanced at once, would, probably, in the first moment of surprise, have mastered the seat of government. But they had not gone through half a street, when the front ranks were separated from the rear, and the stragglers from the rear forgot everything but assassination and plunder. While Emmett was endeavouring to form his followers into something like order, he received intelligence of the murder of Lord Kilwarden. He hastened to the scene of outrage; and, when he beheld the result, at once abandoned his enterprise. The insurrection was begun and ended in less than two hours. We have conversed with many citizens of Dublin contemporary with the event, who were quite unconscious that any attempt had been made on the government, until they read the account in the newspapers on the following morning. No one can fail to see that this lame and impotent conclusion was inevitable from the beginning, if he has examined Emmett's own plan of attack, recently published by

Dr. Madden, in his history of the United Irishmen. It is a sad illustration of the perils which civilians encounter, when playing at soldiers; his only chance was that which he ultimately embraced – to push forward direct to the Castle, and trust the rest to fortune. But he formed a plan which required disciplined soldiers and experienced leaders; he committed the grievous fault of taking everything for granted, and when the moment of action arrived, as he himself informs us, nothing was ready.

Alarm was raised when danger was over: O'Connell appeared in arms, to support the government, as a member of the lawyers' corps of yeomanry, and, according to his son's account, exerted himself to save the people from the military outrages with which they were menaced by the terrified partisans of the ascendancy. Others, however, assert that he was most exuberant in his loyalty on the occasion, and that he lent efficient aid in delivering over the insurgents to the vengeance of the law.

A romantic interest is thrown over Emmett's case by his passionate attachment to Miss Curran, which was fully returned. It is, indeed, believed that he could have made his escape, had he not lingered about Dublin, in the hope of obtaining a parting interview. Though much inquiry was made on the subject, all research completely failed to discover by whom the young man was betrayed to Major Sirr; but his capture must be attributed rather to his own neglect of ordinary precautions than to any deliberate treachery. We have recently been put in possession of a correct copy of the remarkable speech which Emmett delivered before sentence of death was pronounced. We shall quote the concluding paragraph:– 'My lord, you are impatient for the sacrifice. The blood which you seek is not congealed by the artificial terrors which surround your victim; it circulates warmly and unruffled through its channels, and in a little time it will cry to Heaven. Be yet patient! I have but a few words more to say – I am going to my cold and silent grave – my lamp of life is nearly extinguished – I have parted with everything that was dear to me in this life, and for my country's cause, with the idol of my soul, the object of my affections. My race is run – the grave opens to receive me, and I sink into its bosom. I have but one request to ask at my departure from this world – it is *the charity of its silence*. Let no man write my epitaph; for as no man who knows my motives dare now vindicate them, let not prejudice or ignorance asperse them. Let them rest in obscurity and peace, my memory be left in oblivion, and my tomb remain uninscribed, until other times and other men can do justice to my character. When my country takes her place among the nations of the earth, than, and not till then, let my epitaph be written. I have done.'

This speech effected what few efforts of eloquence could have accomplished – it shook the firm nerves of Toler, Lord Norbury. For the first and last time in his life, he exhibited symptoms of emotion in pronouncing sentence of death upon a prisoner. Emmett, however, met his doom unmoved, and seemed to take a pride in rejecting sympathy and commiseration; his end was that of one who had little regret for the past, and bright hopes for futurity.

Sympathy for this young man's fate by no means implies approbation of his cause. Indeed, none felt more for him than the members of the government he had endeavoured to overthrow. Even the speech which Mr. (since Lord) Plunkett delivered to the jury, while it denounced his attempt, did justice to the purity of his personal character. Intentions alone are not sufficient to confer the title of patriot; and we think that Emmett had as imperfect a conception of the end at which he aimed, as he had of the adequacy of the means by which it was to be effected. He speaks, in the paper to which we have already referred, of a thousand pounds as a sufficient supply of money, and of a thousand men as an adequate army. He trusted to the chance of success, for the means by which the success was to be achieved. He had resolved to overthrow the

British government in Ireland, but he never appears to have considered what form of government he would erect in its place. He talked, indeed, of a provisional government, with defined and limited powers, but did not know of what materials it could be framed. Ardent young men, impatient of real or imaginary grievances, are anxious to destroy existing institutions, without considering that they have no right to pull down until they have settled what to build up. The destructive and constructive faculties are very different in their nature. We respect Washington and Franklin not so much for having resisted England, as for having organized America. We do not refuse pity to Emmett, but can accord him little more. He was inadequate to the task he had undertaken; and only added a lamentable illustration to the many proofs of the aphorism, that patriotism is pernicious to the objects of its choice when it is not accompanied and tempered by prudence.

This was the view which O'Connell took of this event; later circumstances brought him into contact with some who had taken a share in the insurrections of 1798 and 1803; he always denounced both attempts, as most injurious to the cause which they were designed to serve; and when remonstrating against the imprudence into which younger associates were often betrayed, he quoted to them the lamentable fate of Robert Emmett, and the miserable result of his insane attempt, both as a warning and as an example.

Pitt returned to power; but instead of stipulating for any favour to the Catholics, he fettered himself by a promise not to disturb the prejudices of the royal conscience. He even refused to present the petition which had been entrusted to his charge by the Catholic body. His late Majesty, King William IV, when speaking, as Duke of Clarence, on the Catholic question, in 1829, more than insinuated that Pitt could have redeemed his pledges to the Irish nation, had he not been actuated by jealousy of Fox, whom he was unwilling to admit into his cabinet with a substantive share of power. Fox presented the petition, but the motion to take it into consideration was lost by a majority of more than two hundred.

O'Connell had married privately in June 1802: his uncle was displeased with the match, and withdrew from him the aid which had formerly been extended. Feeling sensibly his responsibilities as a husband and father, he devoted himself to the study of law with a zeal and diligence which nothing but a frame of iron could support. At the first dawn of day in summer, and by the light of a glimmering taper in winter, he might be seen daily entering his solitary library, and seating himself at his task before a characteristic piece of furniture, a crucifix and holy-water vase; after a few moments of silent devotion, he bent himself to the study of the law, sanctified by the presence of the symbol of religion. By these labours he soon became one of the best pleaders at the Irish bar: his professional reputation extended, and his emoluments were proportionately increased.

When breakfast was over, his burly form excited attention, as he moved towards the Four Courts, at a pace which compelled panting attorneys to toil after him in vain. His umbrella, shouldered like a pike, was invariably his companion; the military step which he had acquired in the yeomanry, strangely blended with the trot characteristic of an active sportsman on the mountains of Kerry, gave him the appearance of a Highland chieftain – a similarity increased, when his celebrity as an agitator began to ensure him a 'tail' of admiring followers whenever he appeared in public.

In 1806 Mr. O'Connell first began to take an active part in Catholic affairs; he opposed and defeated the great Catholic leader, Mr. John Keogh, on the question of petitioning Parliament in that year. On the dismissal of the Whigs, in 1807, for proposing to allow Catholics to hold commissions in the army, O'Connell shared in the indignation, but not in the despair, with which the intelligence was received in Ireland. In advocating the presentation of the

Catholic petition, in 1808, he assailed the new ministry very bitterly, and introduced into his speech some of that personal vituperation which was the greatest blot on his oratory, and not unfrequently a serious impediment to the success of his cause. 'I am ready', he said, 'to admit that the present administration are personal enemies of the Catholic cause; yet, if the Catholics continue loyal, firm and undivided they have little to fear from the barren eloquence of the ex-advocate, Percival, or the frothy declamations of the poetaster Canning; they may meet with equal contempt the upstart pride of the Jenkinsons, and with more than contempt the pompous inanity of Lord Castlereagh, who may well be permitted to hate the country that gave him birth, to her own annihilation.'

Hitherto Mr. O'Connell might be considered as belonging to that party which, at a subsequent period of his career, he used to stigmatize bitterly, as that of the Orange Catholics; but the dismissal of the Grey and Grenville administration greatly abated the fervour of his royalist feelings; and the tameness with which the Catholic aristocracy of Ireland seemed to endure their exclusion from the pale of the constitution, diminished in an equal proportion his sympathies with that body. From the first time that he tasted the sweets of rapturous applause, bestowed by an enthusiastic multitude on his speech advocating a Repeal of the Union, in 1810, he felt that it was his vocation to become an agitator, and he thenceforward organized the force of democratic movement, to impel forward his favourite measure.

The Catholic Committee became every year more popular in its construction, as the middle classes began to take a deeper interest in the question of emancipation; and as the strength of the democracy increased, the leadership of O'Connell became more decided. Percival's ministry became alarmed at this new phase of agitation, and recklessly plunged into what must be called an undignified squabble with the Catholic leaders. Wellesley Pole, then secretary for Ireland, addressed a circular letter to the magistrates of the country, commanding them to put in force the Convention act, which prohibited the election of delegates; and Alderman Darley was sent as a magistrate, to disperse the Catholic Committee. This was done in a very temperate manner; but the Catholic leaders, resolved to bring the right of interference to trial, held a second meeting on the 9th of July, 1811, in which several resolutions were adopted, designed to set the government at defiance. O'Connell, who happened on that day to be engaged in a cause of considerable importance, did not arrive until the proceedings had nearly concluded, and he thus escaped being included in the prosecution which was commenced against several of the gentlemen who had attended the meeting. They were arrested under the warrant of Lord-Chief-Justice Downes; and they, in turn, gave notice of action against Downes. Dr. Sheridan was the first of the traversers brought to trial, and he was acquitted. The prosecutors resolved to be more careful on the next occasion: a jury was carefully packed from a list supplied by Sir Charles Saxton; and though the traversers challenged the array, and proved the unfairness of the panel, by the evidence of the crown-solicitor himself, the case was allowed to go to trial before this very jury. Mr. Kerwan, the second of the traversers, was found guilty: but the government was ashamed of success thus obtained; he was allowed to go at large on his own recognizance, and was never called up for judgment.

On the formation of the regency, in consequence of the mental incapacity of George III, the hopes of the Catholics were raised to the highest, as the regent, when Prince of Wales, had pledged himself to their cause. When, on the formation of the Fox administration, in 1806, the Catholics, seeing their friends in power, were about to urge their claims, the Duke of Bedford, then lord-lieutenant, and Mr. George Ponsonby, then lord-chancellor of Ireland, were authorized by the Prince to dissuade the Catholics from bringing forward their question at that moment, and to promise that he would admit their claims, whenever he had power. A promise was also given, personally, to Lords Fingal, Petre, and Clifden, when they visited the Prince at Carlton House. The delay of the performance of this pledge was at first attributed to the restrictions imposed on the regent, and then to the influence of Mr. Percival; but when, on the assassination of that minister, a new cabinet was formed, hostile to the Catholic claims, the Irish were filled with sorrow and indignation; especially as the defeat of the attempt to form an administration favourable to their claims was attributed to the venerated Earl of Moira.

Lords Grey and Grenville would have been placed at the head of affairs in 1812, had they not insisted on reforming the royal household. They were aware that the Prince Regent was under the influence of a mistress, and a *convenient* husband, who had more power over his mind than his ministers; and they refused to enter the cabinet so long as the Hertford family held possession of the closet. Earl Moira, to whom the negotiation had been entrusted, indulged in those feelings of courtly chivalry which moralists stigmatize by the name of criminal connivance; he refused to place any restraint upon the amorous predilections of the Prince, and Ireland was sacrificed to a worthless woman, whose only claim to respect was her title.

O'Connell assuredly must be pardoned for having denounced such proceedings with all the powers of his fervid eloquence; but the Catholics cannot be acquitted of imprudence for having adopted the 'witchery' resolutions, which proclaimed the scandal to Europe. These resolutions derive their name from the fourth, which we must quote – 'That, from authentic documents now before us, we learn, with deep disappointment and anguish, how cruelly the promised boon of Catholic freedom has been intercepted by the fatal *witchery* of an unworthy secret influence, hostile to our fairest hopes, spurning alike the sanctions of public and private virtue, the demands of personal gratitude, and the sacred obligations of plighted honour'.

On this pregnant text O'Connell delivered a long and eloquent discourse, in which he lashed, with unsparing severity, the Regent, Lady Hertford, and all the members of the new ministry. This offence was never forgiven; sixteen years afterwards, George III made it a condition of his consent to Catholic Emancipation, that O'Connell should not be allowed to take his seat as member for Clare.

On the 22nd of June, Mr. Canning, in the House of Commons, proposed a resolution, pledging the House to take the Catholic claims into consideration early in the next session, with a view to their satisfactory and final adjustment; which was carried by a majority of 119. A similar resolution proposed by the Marquis of Wellesley was lost in the House of Commons, but only by a majority of one. Such a result seemed to promise speedy triumph, but the Prince Regent, who was more inveterately hostile to the Catholics even than his father, joined the ascendancy-portion of the cabinet, and dissolved the parliament.

The struggle was now transferred to the hustings, and the most strenuous efforts were made by the government and its agents to obtain the return of men opposed to concession. The Duke of Richmond, who was at the period lord-lieutenant of Ireland, exerted all the influence of his high office against liberal candidates; and many Catholics voted against the supporters of their cause, particularly at Newry, where the celebrated Curran was defeated. Mr. Lawless, subsequently better known as 'Jack Lawless', proposed that the Catholic Board should pass a vote of censure on the Catholics who had thus acted: O'Connell opposed the proposition on the ground that the Board had no right to exert an inquisitorial power over the exercise of individual rights; but Lawless prevailed, and thus an element of discord was introduced into the Catholic body at the moment when unity was most valuable.

Further signs of disunion became apparent at the beginning of 1813: the Catholics of England, and a large body of the Catholic aristocracy and gentry of Ireland, viewed with dislike such rash proceedings as the adoption of 'the witchery resolutions', and lamented the violent and intemperate language too often used at the Catholic Board. Mr. O'Connell, who was himself one of the chief delinquents, not only defended the use of intemperate language, but made a sharp attack on the eminent Catholic barrister, Mr. Charles Butler, whose private character and public reputation had greatly tended to advance the cause of emancipation in England.[5] O'Connell also complained that Mr. Grattan had exclusively consulted Mr. Charles Butler in framing the bill for Catholic Emancipation, and had not admitted any Catholic into his confidence. Finally, he had the imprudence to go out of his way to affront the Prince Regent at this crisis, by proposing an address to the Princess of Wales on her escape from the charges which had been brought against her.

Mr. Grattan's motion for leave to bring in the Emancipation bill was affirmed by a majority of forty. No sooner, however, was the bill printed and its contents made known, than O'Connell published a most captious and spiteful criticism on its details, which, though little noticed in Ireland, placed a mischievous weapon in the hands of the opponents of the bill in England. A fiercer discussion was raised on the ecclesiastical clauses or 'securities', as they were termed, by which the king or lord-lieutenant, aided by a Board of Commissioners, would have a qualified *veto* on the appointment of prelates and other Catholic dignitaries, while a second Board should have a right of inspecting all correspondence with the see of Rome. A similar arrangement had been proposed to

Mr. Pitt by the Catholic prelates themselves, in 1799, but now they denounced them in strong terms; and their representative in England, the Rev. Dr. Milner, who had previously expressed his approbation of the securities, not only withdrew his assent, but addressed a circular to the members of parliament, reprobating the bill in unmeasured language and unseemly temper. When the House went into committee on the bill, the speaker (Abbot, afterwards Lord Colchester) moved that Catholics should be excluded from seats in parliament; and this having been carried by a majority of four, the friends of the measure withdrew it, as the leading clause was lost.

This result, mainly attributable to the interference of Dr. Milner and the imprudence of the more violent Irish agitators, gave rise to a fierce controversy in the Catholic body, which delayed the success of emancipation for more than a quarter of a century. As this controversy forms a leading feature in O'Connell's career, we shall briefly state its nature and its consequences.

It must, in the first place, be remarked that the *veto* had no proper or natural connection with the question of emancipation; the former related purely to the clerical body, the latter was exclusively confined to the laity; it was, therefore, unfair to require any sacrifice whatever from the Catholic hierarchy, to purchase political privileges for the Catholic aristocracy. Mr. Pitt had made no such blunder; he proposed the *veto* in connection with a plan for paying the Catholic clergy out of the funds of the State, where such a security for the loyal and peaceful character of those who were pensioned by the government seems both natural and reasonable. But the *veto* was obviously a limitation of the spiritual jurisdiction of the pope, and could not, on Catholic principles, be carried into effect without his concurrence. This would probably not have been refused: England might have obtained a *Concordat*, like France or Prussia, only that laws exist prohibiting all diplomatic relations with the Court of Rome. It is, however, obvious that the *veto*, after all, would be worthless as a security: during the first half of the last century, the exiled Stuarts had the nomination of all the Catholic prelates in Ireland, and yet this power did not in the slightest degree advance the interests of the pretender. As the *veto* would have been useless to the government, so it would have been harmless to the Catholics; the invidious privilege of rejection would have been so rarely exercised as to fall into practical desuetude: in fact, England would have a far greater share in the nomination of the Irish Catholic prelates than any domestic arrangements could bestow, by establishing a diplomatic agency at the Vatican, and stationing a frigate at Ancona. Of the *veto* it may be said, with more truth than it was of Pope Gregory's reformation of the Calendar, that 'it found out an evil which did nobody any harm, and provided a remedy which did nobody any good'.

The Catholic Board met, for the first time after the withdrawal of the bill, on the 29th of May, 1813; and signs of dissension, menacing future and dangerous discord, soon became manifest. Lord Trimleston, on taking the chair, lamented the loss of the measure, which he called 'the Great Charter of Emancipation'. O'Connell, on the contrary, denounced it as a covert means of perpetuating degradation and slavery. In describing the probable composition of the Ecclesiastical Commission, he indulged his unhappy taste for vituperation, and most bitterly assailed Mr. (since Sir Robert) Peel, who had recently been appointed secretary for Ireland. 'Well', said he, this hopeful commission, this 'charter of emancipation', was to be framed by his grace the Duke of Richmond; and upon whom is it likely that his choice would fall? Recollect, however, that before even his selection commenced, you were certain of having, as president of this commission, that ludicrous enemy of ours, who has got in jest the name he deserves in good earnest – that of Orange Peel – a raw youth, squeezed out of the workings of I know not what factory in England, who began his parliamentary career by vindicating the gratuitous destruction of our brave soldiers in the murderous expedition to Walcheren, and was sent over here before he got rid of the foppery of perfumed handkerchiefs and thin shoes, upon the ground, I suppose, that he had given a specimen of his talents for vindication, that might be useful to the present and future administrations of Ireland; in short, that he was a lad ready to vindicate anything – everything.

'This special vindicator was to be at the head of the proposed commission. And let me dismiss him for ever, by venturing to conjecture what he may hereafter be in our country. But, no; I will not, I cannot estimate his future qualities. It is impossible to say what the man may be in old age, who, young – with the first impressions of nature about him – with a heart uncontaminated at least by much intercourse with the world – with any charities of his nature unsullied – with any milk of human kindness unexhausted – whose first step in life was the vindication of the most foolish and the most cruel – the most absurd and the most fatal – the most useless and the most murderous expedition, that human insanity ever directed, or human depravity ever applauded.'

Neither Peel nor the Walcheren expedition had the most remote connection with the matter in debate – a vote of thanks to the Catholic prelates: but we have quoted the passage as a specimen of the gratuitous attacks and wanton personalities in which O'Connell so frequently indulged, and which were often as injurious to himself and his cause, as they were galling to his enemies.

An amendment was moved by Mr. Hussey; it was supported by Sir Edward Bellew, who showed that the Catholic archbishop of Dublin (Troy) had been consulted on the subject of the ecclesiastical clauses by Mr. Canning; that he had consented to them, though with reluctance, and had suggested some alterations in the construction of the commission, which had been adopted. This was subsequently confirmed by Archbishop Troy himself, in an explanatory letter; he only added that the consent was more qualified, and the reluctance more strongly expressed, than had been stated. Mr. Bellew, an eminent counsellor, went further, and accused the Catholic prelates of something like duplicity and covert hostility to the measure. O'Connell replied in a vehement philippic, marked throughout by a spirit of rancour, which, at this day, seems quite too strong for the occasion. A division took place; sixty-one supported the vote of thanks to the bishops, and twenty recorded their dissent.

The conduct of the Rev. Dr. Milner next became the subject of angry debate. The Board of English Catholics assembled under the presidency of the Earl of Shrewsbury denounced his interference as unwarrantable, declared that the charge he had brought against Mr. Charles Butler was a calumny, and expelled him from his seat on their select committee. In Ireland, after a sharp contest at the Catholic Board, it was resolved, by a majority of fifteen to ten, that a vote of thanks to Dr. Milner should be proposed at the next aggregate meeting. The task devolved upon Mr. O'Connell, who fiercely assailed the advocates of emancipation in parliament, the Irish Catholics, who had accepted the securities, and all the English Catholics without exception. Still more indiscreet, and certainly unprophetic, was his allusion to the political aspect of affairs in the summer of 1813. 'Yes', said he, 'the hour of your emancipation is at hand; you will, you must be emancipated; not by the operation of any force or violence, which are unnecessary, and would be illegal on your part, but by the repetition of your constitutional demands by petition, and still more by the pressure of circumstances and the great progress of events. Yes, your emancipation is certain, because England wants the assistance of all her people. *The dream of delivering the Continent from the dominion of Buonaparte has vanished.* The idle romance of

German liberty – whoever heard of German liberty? – is now a cheerless vision. The allied Russian and Prussian armies may perhaps escape, but they have little prospect of victory. The Americans have avenged our outrages on their seamen, by quenching the meteor-blaze of the British naval flag. The war with the world – England alone against the world – is in progress. We shall owe to her good sense what ought to be conceded by her generosity.'

The minority of the Catholic Board absented themselves from this mischievous meeting, which seemed to have been assembled for the express purpose of dividing the Catholic body, and alienating their Protestant friends and supporters. They also abstained from sanctioning the address to the Princess of Wales, which was too obvious a piece of spite against the Prince Regent; and they protested against the depreciating attacks which O'Connell repeatedly made on the character and merits of Grattan. To complete the vagaries of the Board, a proposal was seriously considered to solicit the interference of the Spanish cortes with the Prince Regent, in behalf of the Catholics of Ireland.

Saurin,[6] in the summer of 1813, renewed his vindictive prosecutions of the press, his selected victim being John Magee, proprietor of the *Dublin Evening Post*, then, as now, one of the most respectable journals in Ireland. O'Connell was chief-counsel for the defence, and he entered on his task in a spirit of indignant defiance to the Attorney-General, whom he foiled in the very first encounter, by obtaining an adjournment of the trial. At the trial the traverser challenged the array; but the court decided in favour of the panel, and an anti-Catholic jury was sworn. On the 27th of July, O'Connell delivered his speech for the defence, which is generally regarded as the greatest of his efforts at the bar. Of the Attorney-General's speech, he said, 'It was a discourse in which you could not discover either order, or method, or eloquence: it contained very little logic, and no poetry at all; violent and virulent, it was a

confused and disjointed tissue of bigotry amalgamated with congenial vulgarity. He accused my client of using Billingsgate, and
he accused him of it in language suited exclusively for that
meridian . . . I trust his speech will be faithfully reported; and if it
be but read in England, we may venture to hope that there may
remain just so much good sense in England as to induce the
conviction of the folly and the danger of conducting the government of a brave and long-enduring people by the counsels of so
tasteless and talentless an adviser'.

O'Connell artfully turned the Attorney-General's appeal to the
religious prejudices of the jury, against himself. 'Gentlemen', said
he, 'he thinks he knows his men – he knows you; many of you have
signed the no-popery petition; he heard one of you boast of it: he
knows you would not have been summoned on this jury, if you had
entertained liberal sentiments: he knows all this, and therefore it is
that he, with the artifice and cunning of an experienced *nisi prius*
advocate, endeavours to win your confidence, and command your
affections, by the display of congenial bigotry and illiberality.

'You are all, of course, Protestants: see what a compliment he
pays to your religion and his own, when he thus endeavours to
procure a verdict on your oaths; when he endeavours to seduce
you to what, if you were so seduced, would be perjury, by indul-
ging your prejudices, and flattering you by the coincidence of his
sentiments and wishes. Will he succeed, gentlemen? Will you
allow him to draw you into a perjury, out of a zeal for your religion?
And will you violate the pledge you have given to your God to do
justice, in order to gratify your anxiety for the ascendancy of what
you believe to be his church? Gentlemen, reflect on the strange
and monstrous inconsistency of this conduct, and do not commit,
if you can avoid it, the pious crime of violating your solemn
oaths in aid of the pious designs of the Attorney-General against
popery'.

O'Connell's personal appeal to the jury, at the close of this magnificent address, was very pointed, and ought to have been effective. 'Is there', he asked, 'amongst you any friends to freedom? Is there amongst you one man who esteems equal and impartial justice, who values the people's rights as the foundation of private happiness, and who considers life as no boon without liberty? Is there amongst you one friend to the constitution – one man who hates oppression? If there be, Mr. Magee appeals to his kindred mind, and confidently expects an acquittal.

'There are amongst you men of great religious zeal – of much public piety. Are you sincere? Do you believe what you profess? With all this zeal – with all this piety – is there any conscience amongst you? Is there any terror of violating your oaths? Be ye hypocrites, or does genuine religion inspire you? If you be sincere – if you have conscience – if your oaths can control your interest, then Mr. Magee confidently expects an acquittal.

'If amongst you there be cherished one ray of pure religion – if amongst you there glow a single spark of liberty – if I have alarmed religion, or roused the spirit of freedom, in one breast amongst you; Mr. Magee is safe, and his country is served: but if there be none – if you be slaves and hypocrites, he will await your verdict, and despise it.'

The jury had been carefully selected, and of course found a verdict for the crown. O'Connell's speech was less a defence of the traverser, than a bold and startling assault on the prosecutor, and the Irish government of that day; but he did not neglect any material point in his client's defence; and even if he had confined himself strictly to his duties as an advocate, the issue would still have been the same, for the jury shared the prejudices, and the court partici-pated in the vindictive feelings, of the prosecutor. Magee, however, thought otherwise: his friends, indeed, assert that the alleged libel was written by Mr. O'Connell himself, and that he ought either to have avowed the authorship, or avoided raising the prejudices of the court against his client.[7] Another scene of personal altercation between O'Connell and Saurin ensued, when the traverser was brought up for judgment, and O'Connell indirectly menaced the Attorney-General with personal chastisement. The judges promptly checked such indecency, and he continued his argument in a milder strain. When he concluded, he had the mortification to find himself repudiated by his client, who instructed his second counsel, Mr. Wallace, to disavow Mr. O'Connell's speech in unequivocal terms. Magee was sentenced to two years' imprisonment, and a fine of five hundred pounds; and it is still a common reproach against the great agitator, that he never made any exertions to procure compensation for the losses and sufferings which the unfortunate man endured in the Catholic cause.

In the December of 1813, the Catholic Board engaged in correspondence with Lord Donoughmore and Mr. Grattan, on the course that ought to be adopted in reference to the Catholic cause during the ensuing year. Both these patriotic legislators refused to be fettered by the dictation of the Board in their course of action, while Mr. O'Connell insisted that they ought to be guided by the instructions of the Catholic body. A new source of discord was opened by Dr. Drumgoole, a Catholic of the middle-ages, a black-letter fanatic, who could never comprehend that he lived in the nineteenth century, and who perplexed his hearers to discover by what accident he escaped being born in the sixteenth. He proposed a positive and distinct declaration of the Catholics against all 'securities' whatever, and even against entertaining any proposition in which they should be suggested. Such an impolitic course was strongly opposed by Richard Lalor Shiel, now master of the mint, in one of the most brilliant harangues ever delivered in a public assembly; its poetic eloquence, its rich imagery, its glowing periods, were not more conspicuous than its liberal and conciliatory recommendations, and the prudent course of policy which the orator advocated. O'Connell replied with scarcely inferior power; the meeting adopted his views, and Dr. Drumgoole's proposition was carried. Such, however, was the reprobation bestowed on some violent and intolerant passages in the learned doctor's speech, that the Board was compelled to enter a protest against its dangerous doctrines, on their journals. O'Connell attempted to defend Drumgoole, but finding that the current of opinion was against him, finally acquiesced in the propriety of the disclaimer.

Early in 1814, a new impulse was given to the *veto* controversy by the announcement that the prelates entrusted with the administration of ecclesiastical affairs at Rome during the captivity of the pope, had sanctioned and approved the 'securities' in Mr. Grattan's Emancipation bill of the preceding year. The rescript containing this assent was addressed to the English vicars-apostolic, and signed by Quarantotti, vice-praefect of Rome. An aggregate meeting denounced this document; the Catholic prelates of Ireland declared that it was not mandatory; and meetings of priests protested against its doctrines in every part of the country. The Catholic aristocracy and gentry were generally, however, disposed to acquiesce in an arrangement sanctioned by such high authority: such enlightened Catholics as Sheil, Wyse, Woulfe, and others, were disposed to meet the government in a conciliatory temper, but they were overborne by the clamour of the multitude; O'Connell had raised a cry against the *veto* not to be stifled by any dictates of prudence, or resisted by any force of argument. Such disunion and such violence drove the friends of the Catholics to despair: Mr. Grattan presented their petition, but declared that it was not his intention to found any motion on it during the session. The Catholic Board was summoned to debate on this result, which, as they had occasioned, they ought to have expected; when, suddenly, Whitworth, the lord-lieutenant, issued a proclamation denouncing that body. A meeting was held at Mr. O'Connell's house, where it was resolved to submit to the government, by not assembling the Catholic Board, but to convene an aggregate meeting, to consider what course ought to be pursued at such a juncture. In all the preliminary consultations the question of 'securities' was prominently brought forward, and angrily debated: O'Connell insisted that they should petition for *unqualified* emancipation, while Shiel appeared as the leader of the moderate party, which was willing to conciliate the British parliament by such concessions as would allay the fears of timid Protestants. Sheil's course was sanctioned by the Pope and the court of Rome, long eager to have recognized diplomatic intercourse with Britain; it was supported by the English Catholics, by the Catholic aristocracy and the greater number of the Catholic gentry in Ireland; many of the Irish prelates were not reluctant to its adoption; and the most distinguished advocates of emancipation in Parliament believed that the proposed securities were essential to success.

Against such a powerful combination, O'Connell arrayed the passions of the priests and the prejudices of the people; both of which were greatly aggravated by the delay of the measure of emancipation, and by the arguments used in opposition to concession. It was O'Connell's belief that the hostility of the Prince Regent, the Duke of York, and the Tory party, could not be overcome by any equitable arrangement which could possibly be devised; he therefore believed that emancipation would not be conceded until some perilous crisis would compel the government to conciliate the Irish people. In 1813, as we have seen, he trusted to the hazards of the war, which then seemed certain to terminate by laying all Europe prostrate at the feet of Buonaparte; at a later period he sought an alliance with the English radicals; and, to the very last, had no confidence in the increasing intelligence of the country, and the justice of the imperial parliament. The two great errors of his career were that he opposed the *veto* on religious grounds, which, if valid, would go far to justify the exclusion of Catholics from parliament; and that he attributed to the English people the obstinacy and bigotry of the Liverpool and Sidmouth administrations. If it would have been dangerous to allow Protestants to interfere with the discipline and government of the Catholic church, it must have been equally dangerous to allow Catholics to interfere with the discipline and government of the Protestant church; and this they must do as members of parliament, for the Anglican church is a parliamentary establishment.[8] This consequence did not escape the acute intelligence of O'Connell; but whenever it was pressed upon his notice, as we know that it was at the period of which we write, both privately and publicly, he evaded it by violently assailing Henry VIII and the English Reformation. This introduction of theological controversy into political discussion, served only to exasperate prejudices, and to weaken the chance of making converts. Still more impolitic was the continued abuse of the English people. There was a rapid growth of opinion in favour of Catholic emancipation, produced mainly by Moore's melodies, which O'Connell checked, if he did not destroy. Emancipation was more popular in England from 1813 to 1819, than from the latter year to 1829. Moore's songs had brought the wrongs of Ireland within the range of female sympathy; lords might vote against emancipation in the senate, but ladies reversed their decision in the drawing-room. There was not a piano in the empire which did not refute the anti-Catholic sermons of grave divines, and overthrow the legal arguments of antiquated chancellors. Liberality became a fashion; all the rising young men of the country were won to the Catholic cause by fair vocalists pouring forth 'the thoughts that breathe, and words that burn' of the sweetest poet and purest patriot that Ireland ever produced, or England ever saw. We refuse not to O'Connell the praise of having carried emancipation by a bold stroke in 1829, but we must not withhold blame for a course of conduct which had delayed its success for at least ten years. Few even of its opponents were at any time unconvinced that its final success was inevitable.

In 1815 the folly of the opponents of the *veto* reached its highest point: at the instigation of O'Connell, the management of the Catholic cause in parliament was taken from Mr. Grattan, its old, tried, and consistent friend; the presentation of the Irish petition was entrusted to Sir Henry Parnell, who performed the invidious task with obvious reluctance. In the debate on the question of taking the Catholic claims into consideration, Mr. Grattan said – 'I condemn those applications for unqualified emancipation. I am sorry that in doing so, I have offended some gentlemen; but my conviction is, that such a proposition cannot pass. When they desire emancipation without conditions, they ask two things – first that they should obtain their object, and secondly, that they should not obtain it; for they put their demand in a shape which must ensure its rejection. If I had flattered the Catholics, and told them, – 'you have a right to make this demand, urge it, and you will succeed' – I should have deceived the Catholics. I have supported their question *with a desperate fidelity*. I do not mean by *desperate*, that my zeal would lead me into any unworthy or unconstitutional compromise, but that it has always sustained me, even when there was no hope of success. Unless the Catholics come to this house in a spirit of conciliation, they will not succeed. I told them so before. I will go farther and say, that conciliation is not only necessary to their interests, but essential to their duty, to the duty which they owe to the state, and the duty which they owe one another. *If they do not succeed, it will not be owing to any illiberality in the Protestants, but to a want of moderation in themselves.* If they do not succeed, their want of success will arise from their want of discretion. I regard the Catholic body with sentiments of strong attachment.

The warmth of young minds may have betrayed some of them into errors, which I regret as injurious to their cause; but unless conciliation is adopted, nothing can be of any use.'

No better proof could be given of the impolicy of the course pursued by the Catholic Board, than the result of Sir Henry Parnell's motion; it was rejected by a majority of eighty-one in the very parliament which had previously sanctioned a similar motion of Mr. Grattan's, by a majority of forty, just two years before. Many bitter reproaches were addressed to Mr. O'Connell by the moderate Catholics, at this obvious consequence of his intemperance: he replied, 'that he was an agitator with ulterior views, and that every year's delay of emancipation increased the chances of obtaining that repeal of the Union which was his remote object.'[9] This reply was not satisfactory to the Catholic aristocracy and gentry; the Catholics of the county of Roscommon presented an address to Mr. Grattan, and animadverted strongly upon the ingratitude with which he had been treated.

A more legitimate object of O'Connell's splenetic attacks was the Orange Corporation of the city of Dublin – about the most corrupt, bigoted, and contemptible body in the empire: he lost no opportunity of holding 'the beggarly corporation', as he styled that body, to the scorn and hatred of the empire; and they laboured in their vocation to supply him with abundant materials for ridicule and indignation. It was therefore natural that enmity to O'Connell would be deemed a qualification for corporate office, and Mr. J. N. D'Esterre, who was a candidate for the office of city-sheriff, resolved to ensure his election by fastening a quarrel on the vituperative agitator.

Mr. D'Esterre was a gentleman of pleasing manners and liberal feelings; as representative of the Guild of Merchants, he had actually opposed the resolution which had provoked the offensive comments of O'Connell,[10] and on more than one occasion he had

given utterance to liberal sentiments, far from being in accord with
those of his brother corporators. But D'Esterre had been a soldier,
and had obtained just reputation for his bravery as an officer of
marines; it was further said that he was 'a dead shot', and could
snuff a candle with a pistol-ball at the distance of twenty paces. We
do not believe that he could have accomplished any such feat except
by chance; he was too passionate to be steady – too hot-headed to
be cautious. Instigated by those who winced under the contemptuous sneers of O'Connell, D'Esterre demanded that the offensive
terms applied to the corporation, of which he was a member, should
be retracted: O'Connell sent back a positive but temperate refusal.
D'Esterre persevered in his demand, and menaced O'Connell
with personal chastisement in the streets;[11] while O'Connell, who
was far the more powerful man, paraded the streets of Dublin,
without encountering his adversary. This rather braggart scene
continued from Thursday, the 17th of January, to the following
Wednesday, when D'Esterre at length sent a formal challenge,
which was accepted.[12]

The parties met in a plot of ground forming part of the
Ponsonby demesne, about twelve miles from Dublin, on the even-
ing of the same day; Major M'Namara, the present member for
Clare, was O'Connell's second – Mr. D'Esterre was attended by
Sir Edward Stanley. During the arrangement of the preliminaries,
Mr. D'Esterre took occasion to say that his quarrel with Mr.
O'Connell was not of a religious nature, and that he had no animosity whatever towards the Catholics or their leaders. The parties
took their ground, and fired almost simultaneously. O'Connell
escaped uninjured – D'Esterre fell mortally wounded; he survived
a few days, and then died in great agony. His friends and family, of
course, declined to institute a prosecution.

The secret of the intended duel had not been kept; all along the
road, and through the streets of Dublin, crowds were collected,

deeply anxious for the fate of 'the man of the people'. Had D'Esterre escaped the pistol of O'Connell, he would probably have fallen a victim to the excited multitude; the injudicious boasts of his certain aim, circulated by his foolish friends, led him to be regarded not as a fair combatant, but as a privileged assassin. When the result was announced, the voice of the people pronounced the sentence uttered by the judges of the field in the ancient ordeal of trial by battle – 'It is the judgment of God.'

O'Connell sincerely lamented the death of his adversary: he had no personal knowledge of the gentleman before he met him in hostile collision; all that he learned of D'Esterre's private and public character, deepened his regret for having been instrumental in his death; and we know that the friends and family of Mr. D'Esterre cherished no resentment against O'Connell, but firmly believed in the sincerity of his sorrow.[13]

Soon after this event Mr. O'Connell, at a Catholic meeting, took notice of a subject on which he subsequently acted a conspicuous part, – the corn-laws, which were then about to be enacted. He protested against this restrictive monopoly with great earnestness. 'I cannot avoid', he said, 'as the subject lies in my way, to put upon public record my conviction of the inutility, as well as the impropriety, of the proposed measure respecting those laws. I expect that it will be believed in Ireland that I would not volunteer thus an opposition of sentiment to any measure, if I was not most disinterestedly, and in my conscience, convinced that such measure would not be of any substantial or permanent utility to Ireland.'

During the debate which terminated in the rejection of Sir Henry Parnell's motion, Mr. Peel, in opposing it, made a skilful and dexterous use of O'Connell's unguarded violence: having described the great influence of O'Connell, he read some extracts from the most intemperate of that gentleman's speeches, which certainly deserved any name rather than that of *elegant* extracts.

These quotations had a powerful effect on the House, and greatly contributed to swell the majority by which Sir Henry Parnell's motion was rejected; indeed, it must be confessed, that their violence was calculated to alienate all men of sense, temper or moderation. They were universally reprobated on all sides of the House, and by none more emphatically than by the leaders of the liberal party. O'Connell felt this keenly: the Catholic nobility and gentry pointed to him as the cause of their signal defeat; many even of his own adherents doubted his prudence in supplying weapons to their leading opponent, the Irish secretary. O'Connell had two onerous tasks to perform: he had to retract his excessive adulation of the Rev. Dr. Milner, who had again changed his opinions, and become an ardent supporter of the *veto*; and he had to show that his own conduct on that question was advantageous to the Catholic cause. The latter topic opened the way for an attack on Peel: having stated that the *veto* would increase the power of that 'worthy champion of Orangeism', he continued: 'I do not – indeed I do not – intend this day to enter into the merits of that celebrated statesman. All I shall say of him, by way of parenthesis, is, that I am told he has in my absence, and in a place where he was privileged from any account, grossly traduced me. I said at the last meeting, in the presence of the note-takers of the police, who are paid by him, that he was too prudent to attack me in my presence. I see the same police-informers here now, and I authorize them carefully to report these my words, that Mr. Peel would not DARE in my presence, or in any place where he was liable to personal account, to use a single expression derogatory to my interest or my honour. And now I have done with the man who is just fit to be the champion of Orangeism. I have done with him, perhaps for ever.'

Peel was not the man to bear such an attack patiently; he at once sent the under-secretary, Sir Charles Saxton, to intimate to O'Connell that he was ready to waive his parliamentary privilege, and hold himself personally responsible for anything which he had said respecting that gentleman. Mr. Lidwill, as Mr. O'Connell's friend, had an interview with Sir Charles Saxton; they agreed that there ought to be a duel, but they were at issue as to which of the gentlemen ought to be the challenger. Both parties appealed to the press, and their statements differed so much that they became involved in a quarrel on their own account, which they agreed to decide by a duel at Calais. O'Connell sent a letter to the *Freeman's Journal*, denouncing the whole affair as 'a paltry trick', and regretting that Peel 'had ultimately preferred a paper-war.' Upon this, Mr. Peel took the initiative, and sent Colonel Brown with a challenge to Mr. O'Connell, which was accepted. But the matter had been noised abroad by the press: Mrs. O'Connell watched every transaction with the vigilant solicitude of an affectionate wife, and suspecting the object of Colonel Brown's visit, which indeed was not very carefully concealed, she gave prompt information to the police authorities. Sheriff Fleming at once arrested Mr. O'Connell, and brought him before the Lord Chief Justice, by whom he was bound to keep the peace within the United Kingdom.

The duel, however, was not yet abandoned; the seconds of the parties consulted, and agreed that there should be a meeting at Ostend; but on his way through England, Mr. O'Connell was again arrested on a warrant from Lord Chief Justice Ellenborough, and bound over not only to keep the peace, but to remain in the kingdom. The matter did not end here: Sir Charles Saxton and Mr. Lidwill met at Calais, where the latter received, but did not return, his adversary's fire; and thus this episode was decided. Mr. Peel, who certainly proved himself the most pugnacious of the two champions, then wanted to have a separate duel with Mr. Lidwill, which the seconds refused to permit, and the supplement to the original duel left all parties pretty equally dissatisfied.

If there was but the shadow of a pistol-war, there was a very substantial paper-war between the parties; but no one in the present day could feel the slightest interest in the statements and counter-statements. Some amateur of duelling at the time collected and published the whole correspondence, with the pithy motto, *'For the instruction of those who wish to know how to send or receive a challenge without any intention of fighting'*. Not the least amusing part of this farce was the conduct of the journalists both in England and Ireland; the publicity they had given to the matter, and the care with which they had chronicled the movements of the parties, were said to have guided the police in making the arrest; but they one and all disclaimed any share in such a result, evincing the greatest anxiety to exonerate themselves from the charge of having been accessory to the obstruction of a fight.[14]

The battle on the *veto* question was renewed in 1816: the seceders from the Catholic Board, hopeless of overwhelming O'Connell's influence with that body, resolved to act for themselves, and entrusted a petition to Mr. Grattan praying for qualified emancipation. It was presented to parliament, but the motion for taking it into consideration was lost by a majority of thirty-one. It was, however, significant that this majority was less by fifty than that which had rejected Sir Henry Parnell's motion in the pre-ceding session. The hopes of the *vetoists* were raised, and those of O'Connell proportionally abated, especially as he learned that the propositions of the British government were viewed with favour by the court of Rome. He prepared a remonstrance to the Pope, which was forwarded, but was refused official acceptance, and he procured the appointment of the Rev. Richard Hayes as a delegate of the Irish Catholics to Rome. Poor Hayes was rather scurvily treated in the metropolis of Catholicism; he was pointed at in the streets, and universally laughed at for 'being a better papist than the pope'; his remonstrances were treated with neglect; and when they were so often repeated as to become troublesome, he was very unceremoniously arrested, and conducted by a military force beyond the frontier. This result the discomfited friar attributed to the coming of 'young Wyse, late of Waterford (Thomas Wyse, the present representative of that city) and a Counsellor Ball (now one of the brightest ornaments of the Irish bench); these youths had repeated to Cardinal Gonsalvi, to Cardinal Litta, to other officials, and to the Pope himself, that all the property, education, and respectability of the Catholics of Ireland, were favourable to the *veto*, and that the clergy were secretly inclined to it, but were overruled by the mob.'[15] From our recollections of Mr. Hayes, we should have many scruples in vouching for the accuracy of his report; but if Messrs. Wyse and Ball made such allegations, they only stated what was the simple and notorious truth. A single sentence from the friar's letter will show how utterly he was unqualified by anything but bigotry for the important charge with which he had been entrusted. Speaking of such intelligent and respected gentlemen as Messrs Wyse and Ball, he has the ignorance and assurance to say, 'you may judge of the intrigue, when to the miserable farce of these silly boys is given the importance of a diplomatic mission'. It was in consequence of the publication of this letter that he was so ignominiously expelled from Rome; and he well merited the treatment he received. Hayes returned to Ireland, but was used as one of the broken tools that agitators cast away; he sunk into the obscurity from which he ought never to have emerged, and his very existence was speedily forgotten.

The *veto* was not the only point at issue between Mr. O'Connell and the seceders. O'Connell's great anxiety was to make the Catholic clergy the political leaders, as well as the religious instructors, of the body to which they belonged. On the other hand, the Catholic aristocracy could not forget the humble origins of most of the priests, in the sanctity of their order. Lord Fingal, for instance, could hardly be expected to yield to the dictation, or follow the guidance, of the son of one of his own tenants; and as little could the wealthy merchants of Cork be induced to submit to the rule of those whom they had subscribed to educate and support at Maynooth. This was never mentioned in the whole *veto* controversy, but it was really the point in issue. The aristocracy sought the *veto*, because they hoped that the government would use its influence to preserve the prelacy at least *'unvulgarized'*, – to use the phrase of one who was as sincere a Catholic, and as strenuous a vetoist, as ever lived; on the other hand, the Maynooth priests strenuously opposed a measure which threatened to exclude them from all chance of ecclesiastical promotion. Similar feelings divided the Catholic prelates themselves; we have heard more than one of their body complain that their *caste* has been lowered by the present system of domestic nomination; adding, that though they had entered holy orders, they had not abandoned the feelings of gentlemen. O'Connell's education at St. Omer was narrow and sectarian; in no seminary were hierocratic doctrines more rigidly inculcated; and the duties and labours of his arduous profession, prevented him from having these notions corrected by general reading and literary acquirements. O'Connell was neither a sound nor an elegant scholar; his classical attainments were below the average of a schoolboy; in history he had read little beyond the compilations with which men of large business are too generally contented; and though he had some taste for mental and moral philosophy, it was never cultivated.[16] He relied entirely for his success on his own mental resources, and they were unquestionably vast; never did any man make so great a show with so limited a stock of information. It was not until he turned author, and gave the world his puerile History of Ireland,[17] that men discovered how scanty was the stock on which he traded. The theology of St. Omer, which attributed a sanctity, and almost an impeccability, to the sacerdotal character, was the predominant feeling of O'Connell's life: he honestly believed that the best service he could render Ireland, was to increase and strengthen the power of the Catholic priesthood; and it is therefore no wonder that he received, through life, the zealous support of that body, which is indebted almost entirely to him for its present existence as a power in the state.

But let it be a warning to any who may be ambitious of succeeding to O'Connell's post of Irish leader, that the most bitter, the most wanton, and the most unjust attack on his memory, has come from the pen of an Irish priest.[18] We quote one or two paragraphs, but we recommend our readers to obtain and preserve the whole.

To the Editor of the Nation.

'Il ne faut craindre rien quand on a tout a craindre'.

'MY DEAR SIR, – Upon seeing your number of last Saturday, the first since first I saw the *Nation*, that jarred with my sentiments, the gloom misplaced upon your columns fell heavily on my heart. Whether any section of Irishmen sympathize with my feelings, I cannot know as yet . . .

'Mr. O'Connell's death, in my deliberate opinion, has been no loss whatever to this Irish nation. On the contrary, I think that Mr. O'Connell has been doing before his death, and was likely to continue doing as long as he might live, very grievous injury to Ireland; so that I account his death rather a gain than a loss to the country. He was the vaunted leader, the prime mover, the head and front, the life and soul, of a system of policy so servile at once and despotic, so hollow and so corrupt, so barefacedly hypocritical and so dreadfully demoralizing, that the very organs of the government to which it pandered, laughed it into scorn. That his slavish minions, his selfish followers, or his deluded dupes, should have deemed his death a loss, I was prepared to learn; but that the Irish confederates, whom he insulted, spurned, and would have hanged – the representatives of the manhood of the nation which he was degrading, which he had degraded into brutish beggary – that these should adopt the error, and make it the foundation of a further and more fatal mistake; this was an event for which I was utterly unprepared – a midnight inundation from which I know not where to hope for shelter. All seems confusion, and it is intensely dark . . .

'O'Connell has boasted that he guided us, and his toadies have vouched every word he told us for fifty years. Well, then, let us look about and calculate our obligations for the service. Whither have we been guided? Where and how has he left us? We have been guided, step by step, self-hoodwinked, to such an abyss of physical and moral misery, to such a condition of helpless and hopeless degradation, as no race of mankind was ever plunged in since the creation. We are a nation of beggars – mean, shameless, lying beggars. And this is where O'Connell has guided us. But it will be said that he could not help this. I deny it . . . Unfortunately for his fame and for his country, he was a mere time-serving politician, a huckster of expediencies. He said things, and did them not. He issued orders, and jeered the men who obeyed him, as the powder-monkies of Cork can testify. He patronized liars, parasites, and bullies. He brooked no greatness that grovelled not at his feet. He conducted a petty traffic in instalments. He boasted. He flattered grossly, and was grossly flattered. He forestalled his glory, and enjoyed with a relish a reputation that he forgot to earn. Above all, he was unsteady, because he was unprincipled . . .

'I deny not the good points of O'Connell's character. And if I do not enumerate them, it is only because all his points, good, bad, and indifferent, have been extolled over-frequently and over-much. He was, all in all, *un grand homme manqué*, possessing great elements of greatness, but alloyed below the standard. He failed in his mission, and he deserved to fail in it.'

In 1817, Mr. Grattan again brought forward the motion for emancipation, and the majority against the Catholics was reduced to twenty-four. It was not mooted in the following year, which closed the existence of that parliament, and the subject was hardly mentioned at any of the hustings in the ensuing general election. But that election was marked by an event which we could wish to be spared the pain of recording. O'Connell had laboured, and not unsuccessfully, not merely to lessen Grattan's merited popularity, but to point him out as a deserter of the popular cause. The result was one which he did not foresee, and which he sincerely lamented. Grattan was returned for the city of Dublin without opposition; but after leaving the hustings, he was attacked by an infuriated mob; his chair was demolished; a blow of a stave covered his face with blood, and nearly deprived him of an eye; faint and bleeding, the venerable patriot fell into the arms of his son, and he was with difficulty conveyed to an adjoining house.[19]

This detestable outrage upon the great father of his country brought odium on the name of Irishman throughout the civilized world. We who witnessed it could not be mistaken as to its source; the cry of *vetoist* was the signal for attack, reproaches for abandoning the Catholics accompanied the assault. We do not remember that O'Connell, in any of his numerous speeches at the time, said a word in reprobation of this atrocity; and there is no reference to it in the collection of his speeches published by his son; but that he sincerely lamented the occurrence we happen to know, and it was this circumstance which induced him to acquiesce in confiding the Catholic petition once more to Mr. Grattan. The last motion of that eminent statesman in favour of his Catholic countrymen was defeated by a majority of two only; and as the debate went off unexpectedly, this result may be attributed to accident. O'Connell took a very different view of the case; he wrote a long, verbose, and ill-tempered letter to his Catholic countrymen, advising them to make no further applications to parliament, but to fraternise with Hunt, Cobbett, and the radical reformers of England. Mr. Sheil reprobated this impolitic proposal in a sharp, clever letter, and O'Connell rejoined. Here the matter ended; the Irish Catholics could not be induced to sympathize with the English radicals, and radicalism itself soon began to exhibit unequivocal symptoms of decay: O'Connell did not renew the effort; in the excitement produced by the Queen's trial it was speedily forgotten.

In 1821, Mr. Plunkett brought forward the subject of the Catholic claims in one of the most eloquent speeches ever delivered in any deliberative assembly. The motion was carried by a small majority; and two bills were introduced – one for repealing the exclusive laws against Catholics, and the other for regulating the intercourse of Catholic ecclesiastics with the see of Rome. The latter being a measure of security, was strenuously denounced by Mr. O'Connell in Ireland, and petitioned against by Dr. Milner in England; neither, however, succeeded in exciting popular clamour, and Plunkett delivered a philippic against Milner, unrivalled for its sarcastic severity. 'I have never', he said, 'expected a general concurrence: it is visionary to expect the concurrence of bigotry. Bigotry is unchangeable: I care not whether it is Roman Catholic bigotry, or Protestant bigotry – its character is the same – its pursuits are the same – true to its aim, though besotted in its expectations – steady to its purpose, though blind to its interests. For bigotry, time flows in vain – it is abandoned by the tides of knowledge – it is left stranded by the waters of reason – and worships the figures imprinted on the sands, which are soon to be washed away.' Plunkett's measures were carried through the House of Commons by small minorities, but were rejected by the Lords.

Mr. O'Connell had endeavoured to get up an aggregate meeting in Dublin, to oppose the measure, but he could not induce so many as nine persons to sign the requisition. His conduct, however, furnished the semblance of argument to the parliamentary opponents of the measure, and was brought under the notice of the House, during the debate on the third reading, by Mr. Ellis, the Orange member for Dublin. 'I conceive it clear', he said, 'that the Catholics are hostile to the bill, from the opposition it has met with from an eminent Catholic barrister, who is always considered as speaking their sentiments. Why is that gentleman the acknowledged leader and organ of the Catholic body? It cannot be on account of his family, which, though respectable, is of yesterday, compared with some of the aristocracy of Ireland: neither is it on account of his talents; for his eloquence is but of mushroom celebrity, and is far outshone by the talents opposed to him. What then is it that gives him the confidence of the Catholic body? It is, that he really and truly expresses their feelings and sentiments.'

To this, Mr. Robinson (since Earl of Ripon) very properly replied: 'I am no more disposed to take the feelings of the Protestants of Ireland from the honourable and learned gentleman, than I am to take the feelings of the Catholics from that nameless barrister, that mushroom orator, as the honourable and learned gentleman has called him, who, eloquent as he may be – active as we all know he is – does not, I am persuaded, in the ravings of his eloquence, speak the true and honest feelings of the Irish Catholics. It is on this account, that – although I know Mr. O'Connell is dissatisfied – although I know Mr. O'Connell always has been dissatisfied – and although I believe that he always will be dissatisfied – I have no doubt that if the present measure is passed, it will be highly satisfactory to the great body of the Catholics of Ireland.' Had it then passed, O'Connell would never have attained the dangerous eminence which he reached, and would never have acquired the pernicious influence which he gained.

The defeat of the measure in the House of Lords was mainly owing to the influence of the king. His favourite brother, the Duke of York, then presumptive heir to the crown, denounced the measure in a most uncompromising speech, and the Duke of Clarence, afterwards William IV, though known to entertain liberal sentiments, voted against emancipation, in deference to the royal prejudices. Though these circumstances were well known, yet no sooner was it announced that George IV was about to visit Ireland, than O'Connell was roused to a perfect frenzy of loyalty, which lasted without abatement through the whole of the year. He embraced, with an eagerness which savoured of servility, the advances of the Orange corporation of Dublin, to coalesce with the Catholics in giving to the king a most enthusiastic reception; he refused to resent the wanton insult offered to the Catholics, after these advances had been made, by dressing up King William's statue in tawdry finery, on the 12th of July, the great Orange anniversary; and he vehemently opposed Mr. Sheil's proposal, that the Catholic address to the king should be accompanied by a petition for redress of grievances. Many Catholics remonstrated against this injudicious and servile course. At one of the meetings in the Corn Exchange, Mr. Macarthy said, 'I clearly see that the trick intended by getting the Orangemen and Catholics to appear cordial together, is to show the king that all the reports, which have gone abroad concerning this country, are ill-founded; and when the king will see O'Connell, the Agitator, and Abraham Bradley King, the Orangeman, cordial together, he will conclude that it must be unnecessary for Mr. Plunket to be labouring for the repeal of laws which are not injurious.'

It has often been remarked that Mr. O'Connell ever showed himself more anxious to please the Orangemen than the liberal Protestants of Ireland. To gain the favour of the former, he gave the fraternal embrace to Abraham Bradley King, he drank the pious and immortal memory of King William in a glass of Boyne-water, and he wore a scarf of mingled orange and green in token of conciliation.[20] On the other hand, whenever opportunity offered, he assailed the liberal Protestants with virulent vindictiveness; and no sooner was Catholic emancipation passed than he publicly declared, that the greatest difficulty he had had to endure through the whole course of the previous agitation, arose from his having been compelled to suppress his feelings of hostility to the Protestant advocates of the Catholic cause. His enemies accounted for this by declaring that he felt he could only secure power and profit by perpetuating the religious divisions and dissensions of Ireland. We know that he was actuated by no such mean and mercenary motives; through life he believed that the purity of the Catholic religion in Ireland could only be maintained by keeping the Irish Catholics distinct and apart from the Irish Protestants. A fusion between the liberal and enlightened men of both churches, would, he feared, generate a cold latitudinarianism, such as prevails in France; and this he dreaded as little better than infidelity. That bright ornament of the Catholic church in Ireland, Dr. Doyle, differed from O'Connell on this point, and hence arose that want of cordiality between the great agitator and the estimable prelate, which led them more than once to engage in paper war.[21] It was from the same dread of fusion and latitudinarianism, that he so fiercely assailed the measure for establishing Provincial Colleges in Ireland. It was for the same reasons, that he almost worshipped Archbishop Mac Hale, while he looked with suspicion on Archbishop Murray.[22]

George IV arrived, and was received by the Irish Catholics with the most frantic excess of joy: O'Connell's fervour of loyalty was carried to the extent of servile adulation; he and his followers professed the most unbounded devotion to the person of the sovereign; and the Ascendancy stood aghast at finding itself surpassed in extravagant declarations of passive obedience. Sheil held himself aloof from these degrading demonstrations; he and a few more felt that to hope to win over George IV, by such excess of homage, was less wise than the childish plan of catching birds by throwing salt on their tails. In fact, O'Connell's self-imposed humiliation produced an effect directly contrary to that which he intended and expected: as the king heard no complaint of grievance, and was offered no petition for redress, he very sagely concluded that the Irish were very well satisfied already, and that emancipation was only sought by some obscure faction – a faction which he thoroughly detested, because it had presumed to meddle impertinently with his mistresses, and had taken part with his injured wife.

The hollowness of the pretended conciliation was rendered obvious to every man who retained his senses, before the king had quitted the shores of Ireland. Even at the dinner given to his Majesty at the Mansion House, the standing Orange toast was proposed the instant that he left the room, and received with the most rapturous applause. The king himself was worn out by the passionate servility of the Irish, and hastened his departure. To the obtrusive manifestations of Irish servility, he responded with a theatrical display of sentiment: at parting, he pressed the shamrock, as the national emblem, to his heart – shed a few sentimental tears, such as he always had at command – and left the shores 'overpowered by the acclamations of his faithful people'. It is no wonder that such scenes afforded a precious theme for ridicule to the facetious muse of Moore, and provoked a bitter invective from the sterner spirit of Byron.[23]

But the farce did not end here; at the moment of departure, George IV directed Lord Sidmouth to address a farewell letter to the people of Ireland, recommending peace and unity. This precious document contained as little meaning as could possibly be comprised in so many words; yet, for some months, the Catholics clung to the wretched illusion that this empty letter heralded a change of system in their favour; it was printed at their expense, and circulated studiously throughout the country. O'Connell seriously got up a subscription to build a palace, so as to induce the king to repeat his visit; and laboured to establish a Royal Georgian club, to commemorate the graciousness of the least reputable monarch of the house of Brunswick. At length the bubble burst; the subscription, utterly inadequate to build a palace, was devoted to the more worthy purpose of erecting a bridge; and the royal letter, which in the first burst of enthusiasm had been framed and glazed by thousands of dupes, was deposed from its place of honour, and consigned to the usual fate of waste paper. The Catholics were slowly and reluctantly undeceived, but they could not resist such evidence as the continuance of their political opponents in office, and the more stringent maintenance of exclusive measures and policy. The Protestants laughed at the credulity of the Catholics; Sir Abraham Bradley King, whose clever management had been rewarded by a baronetcy, declared that 'he had taken off his surtout'; the Orange party ostentatiously and scornfully resumed their ancient ascendancy; the Catholics, ashamed of their delusion, and indignant at the deception, sunk for a season into hopelessness and lethargy. In the rural districts of Ireland, the gaudy bubble of conciliation burst more speedily; the peasantry of Limerick, Mayo, Tipperary, and Cavan, renewed their agrarian outrages, and a system of tumult, robbery, and organised assassination commenced, scarcely to be paralleled in the annals of any country pretending to civilization.

In the beginning of the year 1822, the Marquis of Wellesley was sent as lord-lieutenant to Ireland, Plunkett was appointed attorney-general in the place of Saurin, and Bushe was elevated to the chief-justiceship on the resignation of Lord Downes. These desirable changes resulted from the coalition of the Grenville party with Lord Liverpool's ministry, and they inspired hope in Ireland at a time when the country was suffering from famine and fever to as great an extent as in the present hapless season. There was consequently little political movement throughout the year. Canning introduced a bill for restoring the privileges of the Catholic peers; it was carried by narrow majorities in the Commons, but was lost in the Lords: the only reference to the general Catholic question arose from the publication of a letter from Saurin to Lord Norbury, exhorting him to use his influence as a judge to get up petitions against the Catholics; a proceeding which brought down general disapproval on the judge and the late attorney-general for Ireland. The dressing of King William's statue in July caused some tumult in Dublin, and the Marquess of Wellesley very properly prevented a renewal of the obnoxious demonstration in the following November. This deeply provoked the Orange faction; a party of them combined, to hoot and insult the Lord-Lieutenant when he visited the theatre; several missiles, including a bottle and a piece of a watchman's rattle, were flung at his box, and a scene of disgraceful confusion ensued, which was only checked by the interference of the police. The Attorney-General preferred bills of indictment against the offenders, which were ignored by the grand jury; he then filed *ex-officio* informations against them, but the sheriff, who sympathized deeply with the feelings of the accused, took care to place none but their friends on the jury, and they were virtually acquitted.[24]

The Catholic question encountered a strange fate in 1823; on the evening that it was to be brought forward by Mr. Plunkett, Sir Francis Burdett took the opportunity of the presentation of a petition, to deprecate the annual farce of discussion, fruitless of all benefit, and the fertile source of irritation and discontent. In the course of his speech, he reproached Peel with insincerity, declaring that he was too enlightened to be imposed on by childish apprehension of 'the pope, the devil, and the pretender'. Peel, who, at this time, by his admirable conduct as home-secretary, had reaped a rich harvest of golden opinions, made a very sharp reply. This bit of personal altercation was preliminary to another of a more grave and serious character. Brougham, who had come into the House after the commencement of the debate, pronounced a terrific invective against Canning, whom he accused of having betrayed the Catholics, and of having truckled to Lord Eldon. Canning declared the accusation a falsehood. Then followed a tedious scene of soothings, and recommendations, and awkward apologies – after which Plunkett brought forward his motion: when he rose, the greater part of the Whig leaders left the House; and when he concluded, the debate was abruptly but indefinitely adjourned, amid the most admired confusion.

But while the hopes of the Catholics were thus baffled, O'Connell had matured that great project which he ultimately rendered the engine of their success:– the plan of the CATHOLIC ASSOCIATION was formed. Its machinery was devised by O'Connell, and by no other man could it have been so efficiently worked. When he first mentioned it to Sheil his plan of a comprehensive association, including two classes of members, subscribers of a pound and of a shilling annually, that gentleman expressed some doubts of its success, and during the year 1823 it gave few symptoms of healthy and permanent existence. One of its rules required that an adjournment should take place if ten members were not present at half-past three o'clock. O'Connell's plan of small subscriptions had not been propounded in the earlier stages of the Association; and when he had it prepared, he failed several successive days in procuring a sufficient attendance. At length, on Wednesday, the 4th of February, 1824, by pressing into his service two Maynooth priests, who happened to be in the shop of Coyne, the Catholic bookseller, in whose house the infant Association was held, O'Connell was enabled to make up the required 'council of ten'. He forthwith developed his plan: its simplicity and its efficiency were equally obvious; and it was adopted with greater enthusiasm than he could himself have anticipated.

The Association rose suddenly into power; the Catholic aristocracy and gentry agreed to forget their old feud with O'Connell on the *veto* question, and gave the new institution the support of their purse and their name: the priests adhered to it with a zeal and enthusiasm which frequently led them beyond the limits of their sacred vocation; and the peasants, invited to take a share in the movement by the payment of a penny per month, under the name of the 'Catholic Rent', came forward with extraordinary eagerness, to join in the first movement that had ever recognized their political existence. Though the object of the body was professedly to obtain emancipation, its efforts were extended to a greater variety of useful and sometimes doubtful purposes; every complaint of local wrong arising from the oppression of landlords or the misconduct of magistrates, was investigated by the Association, and public attention directed to the subject.

> 'The village Hampden that with dauntless breast
> The petty tyrant of his fields withstood,'

instead of, as heretofore, being crushed in the unequal controversy, now found himself supported by a powerful organization, and hurled defiance at the oppressor. Archbishop Magee, elevated to the see of Dublin by the friendship of Plunkett, whom he had deceived by his professions of liberality, just at this period added fresh fuel to religious rancour in Ireland by extending his bigotry from the Catholic living to the Catholic dead. He and his clergy refused to allow the services of the Catholic church, in whole or in part, to be recited at the burial of a Catholic in a Protestant churchyard; and we have ourselves seen the recital of David's penitential psalms interrupted by a charge of bayonets. The orators of the Association assailed with indignant ridicule those who mistook everything Latin for something Popish; and though the Irish church then and now could show a tolerable sprinkling of bigots callous to contempt, far the larger portion shrunk from the exposure of what they soon discovered to be palpable absurdity.[25]

Emancipation had, previously, few attractions for the peasant. It promised little more than the re-admission of the Catholic gentry to the privileges of their order, and the extension of legal honours and emoluments to Catholic barristers. The association extended its protecting influence to every peasant's hearth; it promised the poor man who felt himself aggrieved, *the redress of the law against the law*; and every Munster farmer who can remember the magisterial administration of justice thirty, or even twenty years ago, can well appreciate the importance and value of such a promise. It offered to the wronged tenant-farmers and labourers – a far more numerous body than the people of England ever believed – assistance in their struggles for redress, from a body which at once comprehended and sympathized with their condition. Hope and confidence, thus infused into the breasts of the people, produced an immediate and almost total cessation of agrarian outrage; the Association and its volunteer agents, the priests, taught that justice could best be attained by peaceful and legal means, and that every man who violated the law gave an advantage to the enemy. The lesson was impressively inculcated, and was, beyond all precedent, effective.[26]

But this good was, to some extent, counterbalanced by much positive evil. There are more Irishmen than Smith O'Brien who are ambitious of the honour of a mockery of martyrdom. Perverted ingenuity was used to get up grievances, and more than one Protestant landlord was wantonly provoked into acts which might bear the semblance of persecution. False charges, even against the most virtuous men, were involuntarily circulated by the agency of the Association; orators at the meetings not unfrequently indulged in what they designated rhetorical artifices, but everybody else called simple fabrications. The bitterness between sects and parties was aggravated by weekly harangues, in which the aim of too many orators seemed to be, to find an excuse for their own intemperate passions by inflaming those of their hearers.

Religious controversy was superadded to other causes of hatred. The Kildare-Place Society, a voluntary association, but supported, to some extent, by a parliamentary grant, undertook the task of national education in Ireland, but made it a fundamental rule, that the Bible without note or comment should be read in the schools. The Catholics protested against this rule as inconsistent with the discipline of their church: many Protestants declared that the Bible ought not to be degraded into a school-book; and all men of common sense contended that the right of laymen to read the Scriptures included the right to leave them unread, if they pleased. But the committee of the Society, most of whom were members of other societies, established for the avowed purpose of proselyting Catholics, refused to alter the obnoxious rule; which thus, generally, and not unreasonably, was regarded as a dishonest means for facilitating proselytism. Controversial meetings on the subject were frequent: O'Connell, Sheil, poor Bric,[27] and several others, met missionary crusaders on the platform, and indulged in theological tournaments, which would have been infinitely amusing, if they had not been infinitely mischievous. There was a regular religious duel, of several days' duration, between the Rev. Mr. Pope and the Rev. Mr. Maguire, towards the close of the campaign, followed by a paper war, which spread over several years. No one was near, to read the passionate disputants that impressive lesson of Edgar Quinet[28] – 'When Protestant and Catholic theologians rush into the controversial arena, calling upon Reason to act as umpire, they should address her as the gladiators of old did the Roman emperors, 'Behold, those who are come to die before thee, salute thee!'

This troubled atmosphere of Ireland seemed O'Connell's natural element; it gave vent to the fiery activity by which his soul was consumed. The happiest moments of his life were those in which political and religious strife raged around. He felt like Samson engaged against the embattled Philistines; but the jawbone he wielded belonged to a much nobler animal than that which the Hebrew champion used as a weapon. Every blow told: one stroke sent down a Dublin alderman; another, a Cork evangelical; and another, a Galway landlord. Two proselytizing missionaries, Captain Gordon and the Hon. Baptist Noel, came from England, to aid in advancing that most incomprehensible of delusions and blunders – the New Reformation; but from the moment they landed they were thrown into a state of perplexity, from which they will probably not recover during the rest of their lives. They could not comprehend that the chief recommendation of all this turmoil (to Irishmen) was 'the fun of the thing': they took everything seriously; and so, in Clonmel, they got savagely pelted, instead of being laughed at like the more mercurial itinerants. Thus passed the year 1824, during the whole of which the Catholic Association practically administered the government of Ireland, and a more noisy, merry, and efficient administration never existed; nor, we must add, an administration more fraught with peril to constitutional government, and the cause of social order.

Aware of the king's prejudices, Canning and Plunkett were unwilling that the Catholic claims should be discussed in 1825, while, with obvious inconsistency, they assented to a measure for the suppression of the Catholic Association. Under these circumstances, the management of the Catholic question was entrusted to Sir Francis Burdett, whose motion for a committee was carried by a majority of four. At the unusual stage of the first reading of the bill, a sharp discussion was raised, chiefly in consequence of an act of characteristic imprudence on the part of O'Connell. He had been consulted in the framing of the measure, but his vanity and his jealousy of the recognition of the claims of others, induced him to address a letter to the newspapers, claiming the authorship of the bill, though he thereby endangered its success. Mr. Tierney found it necessary to disavow Mr. O'Connell's participation; a duty which he performed in a manner by no means calculated to win that gentleman's favour. Two measures, known under the name of 'wings', were connected with emancipation, though introduced as separate bills; one for the disfranchisement of the forty-shilling freeholders, which O'Connell had himself recommended in his evidence before a committee of the House of Lords the preceding year; the other, for payment of the Catholic clergy by the State.

In the debate on the second reading of the Emancipation bill, Mr. Brownlow (the late Lord Lurgan), who had been one of the most violent opponents of the Catholics, declared himself in their favour, and the majority on their side was increased to twenty-seven. A further division took place in the House of Commons, and gave a majority of twenty-two; but before the bill reached the Lords, the Duke of York bound himself by a solemn oath – though rather irreverently introduced into a political speech – that he would oppose the Catholic claims in whatever situation of life he might be placed. The second reading was consequently defeated by a majority of forty-eight, in which was included the Marquis of Anglesey, who had previously been favourable to the Catholic claims.

A great majority of the Catholic aristocracy and gentry, including some of the leading prelates, viewed the proceedings of the Catholic Association with some alarm, and became anxious for the settlement of the Catholic question more through dread of the evil consequences likely to result from delay, than from anxiety to reap the advantages which admission to their constitutional franchises and privileges would open. The members of the Catholic Association itself became alarmed at the extent of the power which they possessed, and afraid of the fearful responsibilities which it entailed. Even the more rational portion of the Orangemen of Ireland felt alarmed by the success of the Association, and were infinitely more inclined to a compromise than at any previous or subsequent period of their history. The Catholic Association yielded without a struggle, and was dissolved; the Orange lodges were equally obedient to the new law; but the speech of the Duke of York, and the rejection of the Emancipation bill by the House of Lords, produced a new series of agitations and excitements, from which the empire will not recover during the rest of the century.

The Irish Catholics had expected an equitable adjustment of their claims; they had come to parliament willing to concede much which they would find it difficult to retract subsequently, and sincerely anxious to make such arrangements as would tend to harmonize the two religions, and to identify the two nations. They were met in a similar spirit by the English representatives, and, as we have good reason to believe, by the English people; Catholic Emancipation was more popular, or rather, less unpopular, in 1825 than it was in 1829; and had the opportunity of settling the question then offered been taken, much subsequent danger and difficulty would have been averted from the empire. Never since then have ministers found England so acquiescent, and Ireland so calm and tranquil.

The tranquillity of Ireland was at an end so soon as news arrived of the rejection of the Emancipation bill by the House of Lords, and of the Duke of York's speech, by which chiefly that rejection was occasioned. The news was received with a burst of indignation so profound and intense, that serious apprehensions were entertained for the public peace; moderate men became violent, and violent men became insane. The Irish had expected Emancipation, and they received restriction; the law for suppressing associations was stigmatised as 'the Algerine act'; vehement vituperations were poured on its authors and abettors, including even Plunkett, Canning, and many other supporters of the Catholic claims. 'The wings' were denounced as acts of treachery, and a storm of reproach was directed against those who consented to disfranchise the forty-shilling freeholders, and to make the Catholic clergy pensioners of the state. Even O'Connell found that his influence had been seriously impaired, and it was only by the loudest professions of sorrow and repentance that he succeeded in winning back the confidence which he had lost.

On the return of the Catholic delegates from England, a meeting was held in North Anne-street Chapel, and it was one of the most enthusiastic ever assembled in Dublin. Sheil, in one of his most brilliant speeches, announced the determination of the Catholics to persevere until their efforts were crowned with success, concluding with an adjuration to that effect, as solemn as that pronounced by the Duke of York. The whole vast multitude, actuated by sudden and simultaneous impulse, rose as one man, and, with the right hand raised to heaven, joined in the patriotic oath. We have attended meetings where there was louder cheering and more ostentatious manifestations of feeling, but never have we seen an assembly so terribly in earnest, so manifestly actuated by fixed and indomitable resolution. O'Connell at once denounced and ridiculed 'the Algerine act'; he declared that he could 'drive a coach-and-six through it', and that he would revive the Catholic Association in spite of its enactments. He kept his word; the law was clumsily worded, and easily evaded; the Catholic Association sprung into life with new vigour and greater power than ever. In their indignation and disappointment the Catholic aristocracy and gentry not only submitted to the leadership of O'Connell, but supported him with an ardour not surpassed by that of his more ancient followers.

A general election took place in the summer of 1826. O'Connell, by his plan of shilling subscriptions, had calculated and organized the popular strength; he resolved to assail the ascendancy in the very strongholds of their power; and he struck the first blow in the county of Waterford, where at first sight success seemed most hopeless. Hitherto the forty-shilling freeholders had been mere serfs to the landed proprietors; their votes and their rent were equally claimed by the lords of the soil; and so completely did the freeholders *belong* to their landlords, that the county of Waterford, one of the most Catholic in Ireland, was represented by the Orange Beresfords for nearly a century. In this very county, where the vast property of the Marquis of Waterford had so long given his family unresisted sway, was struck the first blow for independence. At the instigation of the Catholic Association, a few gentlemen of moderate rank and fortune, possessing no political influence, presented a requisition to Mr. Villiers Stuart (since Lord Stuart of the Decies) then travelling on the continent: he accepted the offer, posted back to Ireland, and announced himself as a candidate for the county, in an address of great ability and firmness, but also of great temper and moderation.

The Beresfords and their friends at first received this announcement with shouts of laughter; calculating, according to the old system by landlords, they had a clear majority of six hundred electors on the register.[29] It is not wonderful therefore that their organ declared, in a stanza borrowed from Peter Pindar,–

> 'Stuart won't do, – he won't, – he won't–
> He can't succeed – he can't – he can't
> He conquer us, the scab!
> He that ne'er ran a race before –
> 'Yes, you're a racer to be sure',
> Cried the Devil to the crab.'

But after the lapse of a few days, they began to feel some alarm: O'Connell wrote letters of exhortation; volunteer agitators addressed the freeholders from the altar on the steps of the chapel after the celebration of mass; the priests declared that those who voted against their conscience and their country, merely to please their landlords, were guilty of perjury; and an active canvass of the tenant-farmers was commenced, without any reference being made to the opinions of their landlords. Lord George Beresford and his supporters lost their temper; in the blindness of rage, two addresses were issued in the name of Lord George, which could not have been more effective in prejudicing his cause, if they had been actually framed by the committee of his antagonist. These precious documents inveighed against the demagogues of the Association, bestowed the most abusive epithets on the priests, derided the religion of the people, and then, in a most insulting tone, demanded, rather than asked, their votes. Justly did Mr. Villiers Stuart put the taunting question—

> 'Was ever voter in such humour woo'd?
> 'Was ever voter in such humour won?'

No sooner did the election begin, than popular enthusiasm carried all before it, sweeping away all ancient allegiance, and all neutrality. On the very first day, Mr. Villiers Stuart had a majority among the Beresford tenantry; the workmen and labourers in the employment of the Marquis of Waterford voted against his brother, for the popular candidate; on the fifth day, Mr. Villiers Stuart had a decided majority, entirely derived from the electors on whom his opponent had relied, which was certain to be largely increased by the electors in the baronies, where the popular strength lay. It was, of course, useless to protract the contest: Lord George Beresford resigned, without very well comprehending how he had been beaten; and Mr. Villiers Stuart was returned, to the surprise of all Ireland, and more especially to the surprise of the authors and agents of his return. We had won a decisive victory before we had recovered from our astonishment at being engaged in such a fight.

A still more extraordinary triumph was achieved in the county of Louth, the representation of which had been long divided between the powerful families of Lords Roden and Oriel. It was received as an axiom, that their nominees would walk over the course. Three days, however, before the election, Mr. Alexander Dawson, a retired barrister, of moderate fortune, declared his intention of becoming a candidate, but announced that he would incur no expense in the contest. Such an address seemed perfectly ludicrous; but no sooner did the poll open, than he obtained such a majority as speedily placed his election beyond hazard. His two opponents, who had started as allies, now became rivals, and keenly contested the second seat. The Catholics and liberal Protestants were amused spectators of the desperate strife between the two Orangemen, regretting only that they had not started a second candidate, and ousted both.[30] Like battles were fought with like success in Monaghan and Westmeath; Wexford would also have been won, had not the writ been issued, and the election decided, before the contest in Waterford had taken place.

The Irish landlords felt their defeat severely, and commenced a system of vindictive retaliation by ejecting, without mercy, all the tenants who had proved refractory. On the other hand, the Catholic association organized 'A Tenant-Protection Rent', which soon amounted to a considerable sum; at the same time, it was very broadly hinted that Catholic creditors would foreclose the mortgages of those landlords who chose to indulge in the luxury of persecution. This was a perilous menace to men overwhelmed with debt, and only nominal owners of their estates; the landlords soon saw that they would have the worst in the conflict: they desisted one by one, and even employed the priests, in many cases, to make amicable arrangements for them with their own tenants.

The success of the Catholics in Ireland weakened their cause in England, where the ostentatious interference of the priests at the elections was viewed with constitutional jealousy and not unfounded dislike. At this period, too, [occurred] the delusion of the 'New Reformation'. Lord Farnham, whom Plunkett aptly designated the 'Peter-the-Hermit of this New Crusade', found a sufficient number of Catholic paupers, who were induced, by food and clothing, to allow themselves to be paraded as converts in various farcical processions. We knew some of these converts, and a greater set of scamps never existed; their Protestant patrons soon got weary of them, for they found that they had a very remarkable taste for silver spoons and other valuables easily secreted. So soon as supplies failed, they went back to their own church; indeed, it was a common jest among them, that they had only 'bid good-by to God' for a season, and would return to him again as soon as possible. It is a sad example of Protestant credulity, to find that this most patent of absurdities was received as a sacred reality in England, was declared the work of Providence, in Parliament, by right reverend prelates, was supported by large subscriptions of the generous and wealthy, was sanctioned even by so cautious a statesman as Peel, and was the chief cause of the rejection of Sir Francis Burdett's motion in favour of the Catholics in 1827, by a majority of four. Long before the close of the year, the bubble was shivered into atoms; a result to which the sarcasm of O'Connell, and the pungent ridicule of Shiel, largely contributed.[31] Peel then became convinced that further resistance to the Catholic claims was hopeless; he privately communicated his opinion to Lord Liverpool, and offered to retire from office until the question was settled.[32]

The death of the Duke of York, in the beginning of the year 1827, followed by the apoplexy of Lord Liverpool, opened the way for the formation of a cabinet favourable to the Catholic claims. Canning, through an indirect channel, opened a communication with some of the leaders of the Catholic Association: he candidly stated to them that the revived prejudices of the English people, and the inveterate hostility of the king, were the chief obstacles to their emancipation; he pledged himself to use every exertion to allay the prejudices of the people, and to win over the sovereign; and he requested that the Association should suspend its meetings, as its proceedings were well calculated to irritate those whom it was most desirable to soothe. This was the substance of the authorised communication; but the agent employed went further; he more than hinted, that as emancipation had been delayed by the Marchioness of Hertford, so it would be accelerated by the Marchioness of Conyngham; upon which some one present remarked, 'Then the Orangemen will have THEIR *witchery* resolutions'.

It would have been obviously impolitic to communicate these transactions to the public; but the secrecy placed both Mr. Canning and the Catholic leaders in very awkward relations to each other and the country, which could not have failed to produce most perplexing results, but for the early death of that lamented states-man. O'Connell had yielded to the policy of quiescence with ready conviction, and also with undisguised reluctance; but, as neither he, nor any body else, had confidence in the feeble cabinet of Lord Goderich, agitation was renewed in the autumn and winter of 1827, so that when the Duke of Wellington became prime-minister, in February, 1828, with Peel as chief of his staff, he found the Catholic Association more formidable and more powerful than ever. In fact, it governed all the Catholic provinces of Ireland with absolute sway. 'The edicts of the greatest despots or autocrats who ever existed, the decrees of the French Convention at the height of the reign of terror, were never obeyed with more alacrity and submis-sion, than the commands of the Association by the willing devotion

of the Irish people'. At the instigation of O'Connell, the Catholics
of Ireland petitioned Parliament in favour of the repeal of the Test
and Corporation acts, and under the same influence they solemnly
resolved, at an aggregate meeting, 'to oppose the election of any
candidate who would not pledge himself against the Duke's government'. When the Test and Corporation acts were repealed, Lord
John Russell wrote to Mr. O'Connell, suggesting the rescinding of
the obnoxious resolution. O'Connell proposed to the Association
that Lord John's recommendation should be adopted; but after a
stormy debate, in which O'Connell displayed unwonted temper
and moderation, his motion was rejected.

A resolution in favour of the Catholic claims was carried in the
Commons by a majority of six, and rejected for the last time in the
Lords by a majority of forty-four. The tone of ministers in the
debate was so lowered, that every one saw that the time of their
yielding could not be far distant; the Duke of Wellington went so
far as to say that he 'wished to see the disabilities of the Roman
Catholics of Ireland removed', and 'that, if the agitators of Ireland
would leave the public mind at rest, it might be possible to do
something.'[33]

The agitators received this recommendation with scornful
derision; they had tried quiescent policy in 1825, and the result
was notorious to all the world. They had tried since, the new policy
of peaceful agitation, and they saw that success was within their
reach. One great effort more was wanting, and it was made at a
county election, presenting at first sight far more desperate odds
than the memorable contest for the county of Waterford.[34] On
the retirement of the Huskisson party from the Wellington cabinet, or perhaps, as we should call it, their ignominious expulsion,
Mr. Vesey Fitzgerald succeeded Mr. Charles Grant at the Board of
Trade. He thus vacated his seat for the county of Clare, but neither
he nor any body else had the slightest notion that his return would

be disputed. He was personally and most deservedly popular, he had uniformly supported Catholic emancipation as his father had done before him, and he was nearly related to the Catholic dean, O'Shaughnessy, who possessed great influence in the county. Still the Catholic Association resolved to contest the seat; for some time it was impossible to find a candidate; Major M'Namara, on whom the Association relied, having refused to come forward in consequence of the obligations under which his family lay to Mr. Fitzgerald.

At this crisis, the eccentric O'Gorman Mahon proposed that Mr. O'Connell should offer himself as a candidate. There was a brief moment of hesitation, before the counsel, which then seemed desperate, was adopted. At length, O'Connell's address to the electors of Clare was issued, and it at once arrested the attention, not only of Ireland, but of all Europe.

A goodly staff of oratorical agitators was at once sent down from Dublin to the county of Clare – it included Messrs. Steele (O'Connell's head-pacificator), O'Gorman, and O'Gorman Mahon; it was soon joined by Mr. Lawless (Honest Jack), and the Rev. Mr. Maguire – better known, in Ireland and England, as 'Father Tom', the opponent of Mr. Pope in the great religious controversy; and, more recently, the defendant in a case of seduction, in which O'Connell, as his counsel, had displayed the highest powers of forensic ability.[35] This oratorical corps was re-enforced by Father Murphy, of Corofin, a clever speaker, a boon companion, and as keen a sportsman as is to be found in Ireland: most of the priests in the county followed his example; and thus, in the words of Sheil, 'every altar became a tribune'. One priest, the Rev. Mr. Coffey,[36] had the courage to resist the popular tide, whereupon his parishioners, with genuine Irish whimsicality, declared that 'they would give him his *tay*'; the joke was a bad one, but its interpretation was worse – they gave him *bad halfpence* instead of their usual liberal contributions, and he was almost reduced to mendicancy. So significant a hint was not lost on his clerical brethren, and they became zealous supporters of O'Connell, and of their own pockets.

The history of the Clare election remains to be written; time cannot efface the vivid recollections of the scene. Mr. Fitzgerald appeared on the hustings supported by the principal gentlemen of the county, including many who had been his political opponents. Indeed, he was proposed by the gentleman who had been his rival at the preceding election. O'Connell had with him very few of the gentry, but he had a large attendance of the priesthood. He was proposed by Mr. O'Gorman Mahon, and seconded by Mr. Steele. Mr. Fitzgerald then addressed the assembly: he spoke in a subdued and melancholy tone; he burst into tears as he referred to the services of his revered father, then extended upon a bed of sickness and approaching death; he spoke of himself with unaffected modesty, not concealing that the opposition to his election was equally mortifying and unexpected. So conciliatory was his address, that though the vast majority of the audience were enthusiastic in the support of his rival, they cheered him at the conclusion with a burst of applause which shook the court-house.

O'Connell's address was never surpassed by himself in sarcastic vituperation. His language, tone, and manner exhibited assurance of victory, and measureless contempt for his opponents. 'This', said he, pointing to his rival, 'is the friend of the bloody Percival, and the candid and manly Peel; and he is our friend, and he is everybody's friend.' Unmerited as was the epithet applied to Percival, it was delivered with a force of expression which thrilled the multitude, and even affected those who were convinced of its injustice. He then turned on Mr. Fitzgerald's principal supporters, and assailed them with withering invective, not unfrequently degenerating into downright abuse, but not, on that account, less palatable to the great majority of those whom he addressed.

The election was the most orderly ever contested in Ireland: the Catholic leaders and the priests exerted themselves successfully to keep the people quiet; they forbade them to touch spirituous liquors, and though Father Mathew had not yet appeared, not a single glass of whisky was tasted by any of the peasantry during the election. Some strange events occurred: Sir Edward O'Brien[37] assembled his tenants in a body, to march to the hustings and vote for Fitzgerald; Father Murphy, of Corofin, met them, harangued them, and, placing himself at their head, led them into Ennis, and polled them, to a man, for O'Connell. Father Tom did the same with the tenants of Mr. Augustine Butler. One evening, at the close of the poll, while the crowd waited to hear the numbers announced, a Catholic priest, realizing in his appearance Sir Walter Scott's description of Habakkuk Mucklewrath,[38] ascended the hustings, and in a sepulchral tone of voice announced that a Catholic had that day voted for Fitzgerald. Groans, and cries of 'Shame!' burst from the crowd. 'Silence', said the priest, 'the hand of God has struck him; he has just died of apoplexy. Pray for his soul.' The whole multitude knelt down, and a prayer was muttered in sobs and tears. The announcement was correct; the wretched man was so affected by having voted, as he believed, against his conscience and his country, that he sunk under the feeling.[39] On the sixth day Mr. Fitzgerald resigned the contest, and O'Connell was returned.

The consequences of this victory were momentous: aggregate meetings were held in various parts of the country, at which, many, both of the Protestant and Catholic aristocracy, attended, and took the pledge of the Catholic Association. The peasant-factions, which used to meet for battle on every holiday and every fair, met, under the guidance of the agitators, to forswear their feuds, and join hands in amity. The tranquillity of Ireland was terrible. Mr. G.R. Dawson announced himself a convert to emancipation;[40] the more ardent Protestants formed Brunswick clubs, in which they emulated the violence, without exhibiting the eloquence, of the Catholic Association. Ministers had to choose between emancipation and civil war. The Duke of Wellington, after a long and painful struggle, induced the king to consent that Catholics should be restored to their place in the constitution.

Emancipation had been delayed too long, and was at the last very ungraciously conceded. A stringent act was passed for suppressing the Association; a miserable clause prohibited the Catholic prelates from taking the titles of their sees; and, to gratify the spleen of George IV, the Emancipation act was so worded as to exclude O'Connell from his seat for Clare. Such was the boasted measure of 1829; so concocted as to combine favour with insult – so managed as to show that the favour was extorted, and the insult designed.

O'Connell had declared at the hustings, that, by an oversight in the Act of Union, he was entitled to his seat, and Mr. Charles Butler sanctioned his opinion. There was certainly a doubt in the matter, of which he ought to have had the benefit. His exclusion was as senseless as it was paltry, for every one knew that he was certain of being re-elected. O'Connell was deeply mortified by the refusal, which he persisted, most erroneously, in attributing to the personal rancour of Sir Robert Peel, and the memory of the abortive duel. He was also led to believe that the ministers had resolved to maintain the exclusive policy in fact, which they had abolished in law, and there is no doubt that such a declaration had been passionately made by the king.

O'Connell's address to the electors of Clare was a fierce denunciation of the Wellington and Peel administration; and it contained the startling announcement, that he was about to commence a new agitation, to obtain a Repeal of the Union. His speech at his re-election, which was not opposed, was still more virulent and denunciatory; and on his return to Dublin, he commenced to organize an Association for Repeal, under the name of 'the Friends of Ireland of all Religious Denominations'. The Lord-Lieutenant prohibited the meeting of this strange 'Society of Friends', and O'Connell then exhorted the people to make a run upon the banks, and thus show their power by shaking the credit of the country. A fearful panic ensued; all business was stopped throughout Ireland; the distress of the country threatened universal ruin and confusion; but this palpable proof of the mischief and absurdity of the advice thus madly given, brought the multitude to their senses. The run on the banks ceased, and commercial credit was restored.

Soon after taking his seat in the house of parliament, Mr. O'Connell in 1830 introduced a bill to establish triennial parliaments, universal suffrage, and vote by ballot, but found only thirteen members to support him in a house of 332, while he utterly failed in exciting any enthusiasm for his scheme among the sane and sober people of England. Thus disappointed, he returned to Ireland, and founded a new agitation, on the revolutions of France and Belgium, holding out the latter to the Irish in express terms, as the example they ought to follow in working out the Repeal of the Union. He changed the name of his new Association several times, to evade the Lord-Lieutenant's proclamations, and he attacked the government and its officers with an excess of insult which amounted to absolute raving. All the liberal Protestants, and all the respectable Catholics, refused to share in these proceedings. A numerous meeting of noblemen and gentlemen, convened by the Duke of Leinster, voted resolutions to uphold the legislative Union between the two countries;[41] and during the general election, consequent on the death of George IV, no attempt succeeded to extort from a candidate a pledge for Repeal. The first speech of William IV to parliament, delivered in Mr. O'Connell's presence, expressed the king's grief and indignation at the efforts made to excite disaffection in Ireland: but the agitator took no notice of the rebuke; and the subsequent dissolution of the Wellington ministry, for a time diverted attention from the projected Repeal.

But 1831 opened with O'Connell's setting about his new agitation with renewed vigour. His first attempt was, to have a procession of the Trades of Dublin; then, to get up a new association himself; then, to have meetings disguised as public breakfasts; then, to excite a new run on the banks; and, finally, to hold parochial meetings, where he could vent abuse on the English parliament and people. All this frenzy and fury resulted from a mortification which his own imprudence had brought upon himself. The Doneraile conspiracy, in the summer of 1829, like the popish plot, according to Dryden, was one of those farcical tragedies too frequent at Irish assizes–

'Some truth there was, but dash'd and brew'd with lies';

A conspiracy had been formed to murder some active magistrates, and an informer was found to give warning. In taking his examinations, the magistrates fell into the common error of putting leading questions, which the wretched informer took as suggestions, and he gave them just such evidence as he saw that they wished to receive. Three trials of the conspirators took place. O'Connell was not present at the first, and the prisoners were found guilty; he appeared at the second, and so shook the approver, that the jury could not agree to a verdict; the third had not proceeded far, when the judge pointed out to Mr. O'Connell that there was a fatal variance between the information and his evidence; the prisoners were of course acquitted.[42] Instead of attributing these proceedings to the folly of the magistrates and the vanity of one admiral Evans, who had made some absurd speeches against the Emancipation bill, and wished that they should be deemed so important as to point him out as a victim for assassination;

O'Connell jumped to the conclusion, that the whole was a conspiracy against the lives of innocent men, sanctioned, if not planned, by the officers of the crown, and especially Mr. Doherty, then solicitor-general. He assailed this gentleman with the most violent vituperation, and declared, that when parliament met, he would propose his impeachment. Parliament did meet, and O'Connell, on inquiry, found that he had no case whatever. Night after night he had to endure the polished taunts of Doherty, whose bland eloquence, lively wit, and gentlemanlike deportment had made him a universal favourite; and night after night he had to shift, shuffle, and evade, while the gentlemen around him unequivocally manifested the contempt they felt for so pitiable a spectacle. After this, O'Connell despaired of attaining any position in the British parliament, and therefore sought to have a parliament of his own in Ireland.

O'Connell had simultaneously boasted that he would test the legality of the government proclamations, by bringing five hundred actions, if one of his meetings should be dispersed. A meeting was dispersed, and no action was brought. Government resolved to force him to an issue, and indicted him and others for a conspiracy to evade the law. After trying every possible means of delay, Mr. O'Connell pleaded guilty to the first fourteen counts of the indictment, or, what is the same thing, suffered judgment to go by default, and the attorney-general abandoned the remaining counts. He then entered into a private negociation with government; he dictated the terms to his son, and they were sent with a letter from his son-in-law, through Mr. Bennett, his professional adviser, to be laid before Mr. Secretary Stanley. In this deliberate letter, he distinctly offered to give up all agitation for the Repeal of the Union, if the government would abandon the prosecution, and inform him what measure they intended to propose for the benefit of Ireland.[43] Mr. (since Lord) Stanley, the Irish secretary, indignantly spurned the offer, and said that the law should take its course. The subject was brought before the House of Commons, and O'Connell had again the mortification to encounter the scornful laughter of the House, when he asserted that there had been no compromise, – which was true, as Stanley had rejected every attempt at negociation, – and that he had not offered one, though in the very same sentence he was explaining and defending its conditions.

Ultimately, O'Connell escaped: the aid which he gave the government in the struggle on the Reform bill was too valuable to be unrewarded; the act under which he had been convicted was allowed to expire, and he was never called up for judgment. But he never forgave Stanley for the bitter mortification he had been compelled to endure; and his hostility was deepened by the elevation of Mr. Doherty to the chief-justiceship of the Common Pleas. Mr. Spring Rice, (since Lord Monteagle), endeavoured to effect a cordial reconciliation between O'Connell and the Whigs, but Earl Grey viewed the agitator with unmitigated scorn: he regarded him as a compound of meanness and falsehood, perverting great talents to delude an ignorant and confiding people, for sordid and selfish ends; as a calumniator, who sheltered himself from responsibility under a vow never to fight a second duel; and as a dishonest mendicant, who extorted money from pauperism under false pretences. Lofty and high-minded himself, to an excess, Earl Grey took too harsh a view of O'Connell's failings, and intimated his opinions too bluntly and too openly.

The truce between the Whigs and O'Connell was speedily at an end; he assailed the Irish Reform Bill with the utmost bitterness, declaring that it was both insulting and unjust, because it did not increase the number of members, and give a lower qualification for voters than was required in England.[44] An effective agitation against this was organized by the peasantry; in some cases, the levying of the obnoxious tax was resisted by open force, and lives were lost in collisions. Political agitation sanctioned and encouraged agrarian outrage: O'Connell told the people that it was vain to expect justice from an English government, and thus induced them to have recourse to what he delicately called 'the wild justice of revenge', for every real or imaginary grievance. Whiteboy outrages were perpetrated with impunity, for a reign of terror had been established, which prevented witnesses from giving evidence or juries from convicting.

The war between O'Connell and the ministry was at its height, when parliament was dissolved, and the election for the first reform-parliament commenced. Such was the influence of the great agitator, that nearly half the members for Ireland were nominated by him, and he took care to select none but his near relatives and most servile dependents. These received the name of 'O'Connell's tail'; they were, for the most part, destitute of wealth, rank, or social position: few had any talent, and some were objectionable on the score of character. A greater moral injury was never inflicted upon any country, than Ireland received from this proceeding of O'Connell; the standard of public men in that country was lowered to the level of degradation, and the name of 'Irish member' became a mockery, a by-word and a reproach, in England.

On the assembling of parliament in 1833, Earl Grey introduced a bill for the suppression of disturbances in Ireland, since known by the name of the Coercion act. Its provisions were stringent, but hardly more so than the necessity of the case justified; for the black catalogue of crime exhibited during a single year – 172 homicides, 465 robberies, 568 burglaries, 455 acts of houghing cattle, 2,095 illegal notices, 425 illegal meetings, 796 malicious injuries to property, 753 attacks on houses, 280 arsons, and 3,156 serious assaults. Such were the first-fruits of the Repeal agitation, and such were the reasons why many of us Munster farmers who had zealously supported O'Connell from 1825 to 1829, the period of his true glory, now turned against a man who had adopted a desperate course of policy, which perilled our properties and our lives.

The Coercion bill was strenuously opposed by Mr. O'Connell and the repealers, but several of those who spoke and voted against it, secretly desired that it should pass. Every one remembers the comedy of 'Who is the Traitor?' in which Mr. Hill, Mr. Sheil, and Lord Althorp acted so conspicuous a part, and which ended by consigning the two latter to the custody of the Sergeant-at-arms, to prevent them from fighting a duel against their will. If Sheil, as was reported, had declared himself a reluctant opponent of the Coercion bill, he did not stand alone; Mr. Galway, the member for the county of Waterford, declared privately to O'Connell, that some coercive measures had become absolutely necessary, and he divided with ministers on one of the clauses. For these acts of insubordination, he was subsequently excluded from parliament.[45] Concurrent with the Coercion bill was a far more popular measure, for diminishing the number of Irish bishops, and applying a proportion of the revenues of the Irish Church to the payment of church-cess and other purposes. The discussion of this question became subsequently involved with 'the appropriation clause', which proposed that the surplus of church-revenues should be applied to the education of the people. On this subject two grave errors prevail. It is almost universally believed that this clause was introduced at the suggestion of O'Connell, and that he exercised some influence in prevailing on Lord John Russell to set it aside, in a manner that savoured of political cowardice. Now, O'Connell, so far from proposing the appropriation clause, thoroughly disliked it from the very beginning. Like the Jesuits of France, he was entirely hostile to state-education, and to education of any kind which was not under the direct and immediate control of the Catholic clergy. He warmly praised, both in public and in private, Montalembert, for having supported similar principles in France;

and he joined Sir Robert H. Inglis and Archbishop M'Hale in raising the cry of 'infidelity' against the provincial colleges established by Sir Robert Peel in Ireland.[46]

O'Connell had just as little to do with the abandonment as he had with the proposal of the appropriation clause; it was laid aside in consequence of the remonstrances of the Protestant and Catholic archbishops of Dublin (Whately and Murray), both of whom declared that they would retire from the Education board, rather than stand in the invidious position in which they would be placed by such a clause, with relation to the established church and the Protestant community in Ireland.

O'Connell had often been taunted for not bringing his project for the Repeal of the Union under the consideration of the imperial parliament: but he feared that such a course would be fatal to the gigantic bubble; it was profitable as a theme for agitation in Ireland, but it was certain to be scouted by every man of sense in England. One of the 'joints of the tail', however, revolted: Feargus O'Connor, by the grace of O'Connell member for the county of Cork, was a very sincere, though a most wrong-headed man; he threatened that if O'Connell did not bring the question before parliament, he would undertake the task himself. For this insubordination Feargus was deprived of his senatorial honours at the earliest opportunity, and driven from Ireland to carry on the trade of agitation in England, where he is said to have found it more safe and more profitable.[47]

On the 22d of April the first and last discussion on the Repeal of the Union took place in the House of Commons; the debate lasted six nights: Mr. O'Connell spoke for nearly seven hours; Mr. Spring Rice occupied about the same time in reply; and Mr. Emerson Tennant (now Sir James) exhibited the most striking feat of memory on record, delivering by rote a speech which, if published complete, would have occupied a thick octavo volume. The motion was rejected by the overwhelming majority of 523 against 38, one English member only voting in the minority. An address was then carried, pledging parliament to support the Union, which was on the following night unanimously adopted by the Lords.

The resignation of Mr. Stanley, Sir James Graham, the Earl of Ripon, and the Duke of Richmond, on the question of the Irish church, greatly lessened O'Connell's hostility to the cabinet; he ceased to call them 'the base, brutal, and bloody Whigs', – a choice phrase which had hitherto occupied a prominent place in his speeches and letters to the people of Ireland. Mr. Littleton, (since Lord Hatherton), a good-natured amiable man, resolved to take advantage of these favourable dispositions, and, without consulting Earl Grey, he privately communicated to O'Connell that the Irish government, in renewing the Coercion bill, would not press the clauses which prohibited public meetings. But as the premier believed these to be among the most valuable parts of the measure, the new bill, when introduced, was found to contain these obnoxious clauses. A stormy debate ensued in the House of Commons, and a new schism took place in the cabinet. Earl Grey, finding that the majority of his colleagues were disposed to yield to O'Connell, resigned his office, and retired into private life. Lord Melbourne was placed at the head of the new administration.

William IV was just as much displeased as Earl Grey with the course of policy pursued by the cabinet, and especially with the implied license given to O'Connell to renew agitation in Ireland, a privilege which that gentleman had soon shown his determination to exercise with renewed vigour. On the death of Earl Spencer, which compelled Lord Althorp to resign his office as chancellor of the exchequer, being called to the upper house; the king suddenly and unceremoniously dismissed his ministers, and the fact was briefly announced in the *Times*, with the significant addition, 'the Queen has done it all'. On the recommendation of the Duke of Wellington, the king entrusted the formation of a new cabinet to

Sir Robert Peel, who was then absent in Italy. A special messenger was sent to hasten his return; 'the hurried Hudson rushed into the halls of the Vatican'; Peel posted back from Rome, formed a thorough Tory ministry, and dissolved the parliament.

No one was more surprised and annoyed at this result than O'Connell, and he very fairly took no small part of the blame on himself. 'I will take good care', said he to some liberals in Dublin, 'how I again have a hand in turning out the Whigs to let in the Tories'. His energies succeeded in turning the Irish elections against Sir Robert Peel's government; but, as before, he insisted on repeal candidates: 'Sink or swim – live or die', said he, on the Dublin hustings, 'I am for repeal'. Neither did he shrink from the most violent use of intimidation: he menaced the shopkeepers with exclusive dealing; and, in reference to the election for his native county, he said, 'Every one who votes for the Orange knight of Kerry shall have a death's head and cross-bones painted on his door'.[48] We believe that this extravagance was injurious to his cause, even in Ireland. He and his colleague were returned for Dublin by a very narrow majority, and were subsequently unseated on petition. O'Connell was, however, almost immediately elected for Kilkenny.

The Irish elections turned the parliamentary scale against Sir Robert Peel; after being several times left in minority, he suffered a decisive defeat on the question of the Irish Church, and at once resigned. The Melbourne ministry was restored, with the remarkable omissions of Lord Brougham from the chancellorship, and the Marquis of Wellesley from the lord-lieutenancy of Ireland. An implied contract was formed between O'Connell and the Melbourne party; they were to have his support in parliament, and O'Connell was to have a very large share of ministerial patronage. This arrangement greatly weakened the ministers in England, and did some mischief in Ireland. O'Connell recommended none for promotion but the most adulatory of his retainers: a high colonial appointment was procured for a barrister, whose chief, and, as far as we know, whose only merit was having displayed a pair of stockings on a pole, to insult the Lord Mayor of Dublin, when he went in state to receive the Marquis of Anglesey, on his coming a second time as lord-lieutenant of Ireland.

With this drawback, however, it must be confessed, that Ireland never made more rapid improvement than under the four years of the vice-royalty of Earl Mulgrave, since Marquis of Normanby. It was his misfortune, rather than his fault, that the ministry by which he had been appointed had to encounter the strongest, the most unscrupulous, and, we might almost add, the most unprincipled opposition that ever existed in England. O'Connell was willing, and even eager to abandon repeal, for the more rational cause of 'justice to Ireland', but the Tory opposition having a decided majority in the Lords, and a formidable minority in the Commons, obstructed and mangled every measure, however just or expedient, introduced for the benefit of the people of Ireland. The most wanton insults were offered to the Irish, to their country, their clergy, their creed, and their race. Lord Lyndhurst stigmatized the Irish as 'aliens in language, religion, and blood' – influential journals denounced the Catholic clergy as 'surpliced ruffians' – the reform of the Irish corporations was resisted and delayed, on the avowed ground that the Irish were an inferior race – reverend agitators, like O'Sullivan and McGhee[49], went round the country to kindle the flame of theological rancour against the see of Rome – and the press teemed with the publications of male and female bigots endeavouring to prove that the religion of three-fourths of Europe was offensive to God and dangerous to man. If the Irish had been the least susceptible of races, they could not but have been stimulated to resentment and resistance by such impolitic and wicked proceedings. People in England were not aware of the intense mischief they wrought in Ireland; we know too well that the memory of them still rankles in the mind of the people. In the four years to which we have alluded, Ireland was conciliated to the Whig party, and thoroughly alienated from the English people. Exeter Hall effected what Conciliation Hall could never have accomplished; it kept repeal alive, after it had been abandoned by its author. No wonder when Sir Robert Peel took office in 1841, that he recognized Ireland as his principal difficulty; no wonder that the most eminent of the Irish prelates said to a despairing liberal, 'Be easy, Peel's past opposition will beat his future ministry'.[50]

O'Connell showed unusual hesitation in opening his last repeal campaign. 'The thanes had fallen from him'; no one of the veterans of the Catholic Association stood by his side, save Steele, whose devotion to his leader seemed to be tinged with insanity. All the old familiar faces had disappeared from his councils; the young men whom he had dazzled by the phantom of nationality in 1831, had profited by the experience of ten years, and had become too wise to be duped. One had become a sober clergyman, another a thriving barrister in England, and a third, the most zealous advocate in past times for the exclusive use of Irish manufactures, was seeking to represent an English borough on the principles of free trade. If Lady De Grey, the wife of the lord-lieutenant, had not given some unnecessary provocation, the nature of which has never been explained, it is possible that Peel might have had an opportunity of developing that liberal scheme of policy which he did not formally profess, but on which he steadfastly acted. Lady De Grey was connected with the Cole family,[51] long conspicuous in the Orange party for fierce hostility to the Catholics; but we believe that the impression commonly entertained in Ireland of her interference with the viceregal administration, is utterly without foundation.

O'Connell saw that he had to deal with a new generation which he significantly compared to the 'other king who knew not Joseph'; they were a petulant, conceited race, but among the young men who gathered around him, there was one young man of decided talent and unswerving integrity – Thomas Davis – with whom nationality was at once a passion and a principle, the object of enthusiasm and the result of conviction. Such an ally was invaluable to the sincere, but most perilous to one who only used agitation as a means for selfish ends.

About the middle of 1842 the Repeal cry was raised, and a new agitation commenced. Its progress was perfectly appalling; O'Connell himself was swept onward by the popular current, and, though thoroughly frightened, was unable to find footing as the waters rose around him. Monster-meetings of hundreds of thousands showed how deeply the anti-Irish and anti-Catholic demonstrations in England rankled in the public mind of Ireland. The great agitator found it far more difficult to restrain than to excite public enthusiasm; he was stopped on the road by thousands of impatient peasants, who with reproachful tones asked him, 'Arrah then, counsellor, when will you give us the word?' and had he given *the word*, Ireland would have been in arms, and engaged in civil war, from one end to the other. Though called at the time 'an uncrowned king', there never was a moment in his public life when he was really so powerless. He followed instead of leading public opinion; and when he sought to escape into federalism, he saw that he must either remain a Repealer or sink into a political nullity. If O'Connell were a king, 'the boys of the Nation' – as the Young Ireland party was called from the journal they had established – were the viceroys over him. Until they lost their best man, Davis, O'Connell was afraid of this party; he then fell into the opposite error, and believed that he could crush them by a breath.

He was more frightened by the monster-meetings than the government itself; and though his notorious character for falsehood leaves room for doubt, we believe that he honestly intended the Clontarf meeting to be the last. His inordinate vanity must have been more than satiated by the plaudits of hundreds of thousands, and his constitutional timidity must have been excited by the violence of the demonstrations in public, and the still greater violence of the counsels tended in private. In the midst of his anxieties and perplexities, he was summoned to a sharp encounter with the law. A monster-indictment and a monster-trial became a proper appendage to monster-meetings.

Every one remembers that most Irish exhibition of official blundering and forensic eloquence, the trial of O'Connell and his associates at the beginning of 1844. A jury was fairly assembled, but with every appearance of having been unconstitutionally packed – an Attorney-General tendered a challenge to an opposing lawyer in open court; and, to mend the matter, in the presence of that lawyer's wife[52] – Whiteside delivered a speech worthy of the best days of Curran, Bushe, or Plunkett[53] – the presiding judge delivered a charge as sound in rhetoric as it was doubtful in law – and a trial lasted twenty-four days without abating in interest or lessening to any perceptible extent the anxious enthusiasm of the public.

Before O'Connell could be called up for judgement, he paid a brief visit to England, and attended one of the meetings of the Anti-Corn-Law League in Covent Garden Theatre. He there found that the government prosecution had achieved for him what nothing else but a miracle could have effected; it had rendered him for a time, even more popular in England than he was in Ireland.

John Bull has had a thorough dislike of all constructive crimes since 1794: he thought that O'Connell could not have been guilty of any very overt sedition when it took about a month to establish the charge; he was deeply incensed at learning that the office of an English newspaper had the appearance of being converted into a house of agency for espionage; he was sure that the jury had been packed, and the bench prejudiced; and furthermore honest John reproached himself for having encouraged government to proceed, by feeling too sensibly O'Connell's senseless attacks on the Saxon. This was the general sentiment of the English people; but to the League, O'Connell was further recommended by thirty years of opposition to the Corn-Laws, and by his zealous co-operation in every effort for their repeal, whether in or out of parliament.

Under these circumstances, his reception by the assembled multitude was one of the most magnificent displays of popular enthusiasm ever witnessed. He declared himself that he was not prepared for it, even by the experience of the monster-meetings. His speech, the last of any permanent interest that he ever deli-vered, was one of the finest oratorical displays of his life. He had achieved the object, of which, if he had not despaired, the cry of repeal would never have been raised – he had triumphed gloriously, and completely on English ground.

This event strengthened the suspicions with which O'Connell had long been regarded by the Young Ireland party; it was remarked that he began to speak respectfully of the English people, and to abate the vehemence of his denunciations against the Saxon. The growing feeling of alienation was, however, suspended; on the 24th of May, he was sentenced to twelve months' imprisonment, and incarcerated in Richmond Penitentiary, near Dublin. During his confinement, every possible indulgence was shown him, and on the 4th of September, the decision of the Irish judges was reversed by the House of Lords.

O'Connell was liberated, but he came out of prison an altered man. During his confinement, the presidency of the Repeal Association had been confided to Mr. W. Smith O'Brien, member for the county of Limerick, a recent convert to the cause. The Young Ireland party had selected this gentleman as the rival and future successor of O'Connell, and, during the absence of the latter from the Association, had used all possible means to extend his reputation, and give him influence in the country. In former days,

O'Connell would have brooked no rivalry, but imprisonment had broken his spirit, and had afforded Smith O'Brien time to strengthen himself with his party. Their jealousy was soon pretty manifest; there were bickerings in public, there was marked coldness in private. A project for convening an Irish senate, of very doubtful legality, and still more questionable prudence, was abandoned. A ridiculous club, the members of which were to wear a still more ridiculous uniform – including a fool's cap, the shape of which was the subject of long and learned debate – was patronized by the O'Brien, and jeered by the O'Connell party.[54] The *Nation* depreciated the member for Cork, the *Pilot* assailed the member for Waterford.[55] Thus closed the year 1844, and thus opened the year 1845.

Soon after the assembling of parliament, Smith O'Brien covered himself with immortal ridicule, by courting imprisonment under the speaker's warrant. Both the O'Connells were serving on railway bills; while he, to show the greater purity of his patriotism, refused to attend any committee save one engaged with Irish affairs. He was given into the custody of the Sergeant-at-arms, and, after a short confinement in one of the lower stories of the houses of parliament, was liberated on payment of his fees. The Young Ireland party made a vigorous effort to have this mockery recognized as a martyrdom; but the Irishman's keen perception of the ridiculous prevailed, and 'the Martyr of the Cellar', as the poor gentleman was called, was greeted with inextinguishable laughter, where he had expected unbounded applause.

Sir Robert Peel's proposition to establish Provincial Colleges in Ireland, became a new source of discord between O'Connell and the enthusiastic 'boys of the Nation'. They had no sympathy with the sacerdotal predilections of the great agitator; the last thing to which they could be induced to submit, would be the political ascendancy of the priesthood; they were generally men of education and intelligence, and were therefore anxious for the diffusion of knowledge. On the question of the colleges they manfully stood out against O'Connell, and compelled him, in his own Association, to endure the mortification of defeat. This was the first event which shook his confidence in his own powers; he would have retired from further contest, but for the urgency of his son John, who, to more than his father's bigotry, united an immoderate share of self-conceit. During O'Connell's attendance in parliament during the session of 1846, the insubordination of Young Ireland became insupportable to the chieftain, and he sent his son John to dragoon them into obedience. He might as well have sent a baby to confine a regiment of March hares in a circle of a yard diameter.[56] Conciliation Hall became a hall of discord with a vengeance; after a scene of brawling and confusion, Young Ireland seceded in a body, and set up for itself, under the name of the Irish Confederation.

O'Connell still believed that power was firm in his grasp. 'I will return to Dublin', said he; 'I have the priests with me; and let me see the man in Ireland who will venture to resist the priests'. Bootless boast! the repeal rent, the best test of popularity, began by its rapid decline to illustrate the theory of vanishing fractions; the mob of Dublin looked upon him with coldness; no eager deputations and no bombastic addresses marked his progresses in the country; and in the midst of these signs of declining popularity and power, his country was smitten by a calamity which was fearfully aggravated by the demoralized state of society, too obviously the consequence of his perverse and continuous agitation.

Famine relief, dreadful under any circumstances, was in Ireland perfectly awful; for the condition of society rendered the application of palliative remedies all but impossible. Agency for administering relief did not exist in the country; indeed, it was no small aggravation of the evil, that accurate information was all but unattainable. For more than fifteen years O'Connell had so habituated his countrymen to public falsehoods, that truth, with too many of his admirers and followers, had ceased to be a matter of moral obligation. Fraud and falsehood were superadded to famine; dishonest mendicancy extended real pauperism. The *Packet* joined the *Nation*, in the insane assertion, that it was the duty of the government to feed the people, and even to give them more abundant and better food in a season of scarcity, than they were accustomed to obtain in a period of plenty. No man knew better the wickedness and folly of these insane ravings than Mr. O'Connell, but he dared not resist them, on pain of having the last remnant of his decaying popularity flung to the winds. All his energies were required, and they were honourably and honestly exerted to prevent the fanatics of the Young Ireland party from making the general dislocation of society, consequent on the famine, a pretext for civil war. There was an opportunity for bringing to an armed trial the question of connection with England; and we, farmers of Munster, knew and felt the hazard of the crisis, which appears to have been utterly unknown in London, and even in Dublin.

Thus, at the close of his days, O'Connell proved his patriotism, by sacrificing to the exigencies of his country, that cause, which, however chimerical, had been the predominant idea of his life. Had there been an armed contest, he would have taken service to maintain the Union. But, morally, mentally, and physically, he had to sustain a conflict, which even in the prime of life would have shaken the stoutest constitution. He succeeded in preventing the fatal consummation of folly and mischief meditated and menaced by the young Irish Jacobins; but he paid the penalty of life, for his last great act of political penitence.

The Whigs came into office, but he held aloof from the Castle, for he no longer had Ireland at his beck; he could have had places for his children, and honours for himself, but he forgot self in the misery of Ireland. A broken-hearted and death-doomed man, he quitted his native shores, and his last words, as he left Ireland, were protests against the monstrous absurdities of the two great journals of Young Ireland Repeal – the incomprehensible *Nation*, and the unintelligible *Packet*.

The rest must be briefly told. His friends in London, from the moment that they saw him, knew that they looked upon a dying man. Some of those who had stood by his side in the days before 1829, came around him, and hailed him as the friend of their youth, in whose power it still was to save Ireland by issuing his sane and hallowed advice to the people. It was too late; all that his failing powers could do had been effected: he had survived his power, his influence, and his fame. From the moment that disease laid hold on his iron constitution, he despaired of life, and he yielded to the recommendations of his physicians to try a foreign climate, not from hopes of recovery, but from an anxiety to close his arduous life in the capital of Catholicity. For years before, his family had felt not ungrounded fears that he would suddenly quit public life, and retire into a monastery.[57] When he made his 'retreat'* at Mount Melleray,[58] even Trappists confessed that his asceticism was superior to their own: – it had been his ambition to live as an agitator, but it was the most ardent wish of his heart to die a saint.

Hopes of his recovery were given by physicians, but O'Connell left England with the conviction that he should never return alive. Rome was his goal, but he was not destined to reach it; he died at Genoa, and almost with his last breath directed that his heart should be conveyed to the termination of that pilgrimage which it had not been his fate to complete.

It is not for us Munster farmers to write his epitaph; we have merely recorded what we heard and saw. Our evidence is given, to be estimated by that general public, which can neither be turned

---

* 'A retreat', in the Catholic Church 'is a voluntary retirement into a monastery, for purposes of penance and mortification, during a limited period'.

into a packed jury or a hired association. It is very possible that the evidence will please no party – farmers are usually most unfortunate in this respect – but, what we have detailed is, so far as our knowledge goes, 'the truth, the whole truth, and nothing but the truth', – there is no necessity to superadd the usual adjuration.

APPENDIX I

Athenaeum, 1011 (13 March 1847), pp. 278-9.
The Black Prophet: A Tale of Irish Famine.
By W. Carleton,[1] Esq. Simms & Co.
Letters on the State of Ireland. By the Earl of Rosse. Hatchard.
Ireland, Historical and Statistical.
By G. L. Smyth, Esq. Whittaker & Co.

A TALE of Irish Famine! The stern realities of such a calamity surpass the most vivid pictures of fiction. The novelist should shrink from pourtraying the moral degradation which accompanies physical suffering – the breaking down of the strong mind consequent on the withering of the strong arm – the darkening of the passions which follows the darkening of the hopes – the fierce demands of reckless ignorance for remedies which would aggravate the disease – and the insane vengeance on all who are suspected of combining to disappoint insane expectations! It is not society merely prostrated by suffering that the historian of Irish famine has to describe; it is society dislocated in all its limbs and joints – shivered into unconnected and fermenting masses – having neither the strength nor the cohesion to make any effort for the alleviation of the want – and attributing this aggravation of the calamity to every person and thing under Heaven except itself. We respect Mr Carleton's powers:– no living man better understands the character of the Irish peasant in its strength and in its weakness; no man enters with deeper sympathy into the soul of the poor or more truly reveals the thoughts and feelings that work there. But he could not thus comprehend the secret recesses of the Irish heart if he did not share largely in its sentiments – if he were not at once animated by its warmth and warped by some of its prejudices. The tale before us is neither the best nor the worst of his productions; but it has this striking appropriateness to the subject of Irish famine, that it combines a tale of guilt with a tale of misery, and with much that is excellent inculcates a little that we cannot regard but as dangerous.

The story before us relates to the famine of 1822, – a fearful warning that was fearfully neglected. The personage from whom the tale takes its title was one of a class common at the time – ill-boding prophets of evil, who wrung contributions from the peasantry by the terror which their denunciations inspired. When plenty returned, these wretches disappeared; and in every instance where opportunity was afforded for inquiry into the antecedents of their past life they were found to have been criminals of the blackest dye. The specimen which Mr Carleton gives of the language used by these impostors is not exaggerated:–

Isn't the Almighty, in his wrath, this moment proclaimin' it through the heavens and the airth? Look about you, and say what is it you see that doesn't foretell famine – famine – famine! Doesn't the dark wet day an' the rain, rain, rain, foretell it? Doesn't the rottin' crops, the unhealthy air, an' the green damp foretell it? Doesn't the sky without a sun, the heavy clouds, an' the angry fire of the West foretell it? Isn't the airth a page of prophecy, an' the sky a page of prophecy, where every man may red of famine, pestilence, an' death? The airth is softened for the grave, an' in the black clouds of heaven you may see the death-hearses movin' slowly along – funeral afther funeral – funeral afther funeral – an' nothing to folly them but lamentation an' woe, by the widow an' orphan – the fatherless, the motherless, an' the childless – woe an' lamentation – lamentation an' woe.

There is no class of men that suffer more severely, and in general more undeservedly, than provision-dealers in a season of scarcity. They have what the people want; and their refusal to give it to the people on the people's terms is denounced as a crime. To this popular and most mischievous prejudice Mr Carleton has largely conceded in his portraiture of Darby Skinadre. We take part of a scene described as occurring in his store:–

He had again resumed his place at the scales, and was about to proceed in his exertions, when the door opened and a powerful young man, tall, big-boned, and broad-shouldered, entered the room, leading or rather dragging with him the poor young woman and her child, who had just left the place in such bitterness and affliction. He was singularly handsome, and of such resolute and manly bearing that it was impossible not to mark him as a person calculated to impress one with a strong anxiety to know who and what he might be. On this occasion his cheek was blanched and his eye emitted a turbid fire which could scarcely be determined as that of indignation or illness. 'Is it thrue', he asked, 'that you've dared to refuse to this – this – this – unfor – is it thrue that you've dared to refuse to this girl and her starvin' father the meal she wanted? Is this thrue, you hard-hearted old scoundrel – bekase if it is, by the blessed sky above us, I'll pull the windpipe out of your throat, you infernal miser!' He seized the unfortunate Skinadre by the neck, as he spoke, and almost at the same moment forced him to project his tongue about three inches out of his mouth, causing his face, at the same time, to assume, by the violence of the act, an expression of such comic distress and terror, as it was difficult to look upon with gravity. 'Is it thrue', he repeated in a voice of thunder, 'that you've dared to do so scoundrelly an act, an' she, the unfortunate creature, famishin' wid hunger *herself*? Whilst he spoke, he held Skinadre's neck as if in a vice – firm in the same position, – and the latter, of course, could do no more than turn his ferret eyes round as well as he could, to entreat him to relax his grip. 'Don't choke him, Brian', exclaimed Hacket, who came forward to interpose'; 'you'll strangle him – as heaven's above, you will.' 'An' what great crime would *that* be?' answered the other, relaxing his awful grip of the miser. 'Isn't he, and every meal-monger like him, a curse an' a scourge to the counthry? – an' hasn't the same counthry curses and scourges enough, widout either him or them? Answer me now', he proceeded, turning to Skinadre, 'why did you send her away, widout the food she wanted?' 'My heart bled for her – but –' 'It's a lie, you born hypocrite – it's a lie – your heart never bled for anything, or anybody.' 'But you don't know', replied the miser, 'what I lost by –' 'It's a lie, I say', thundered out the gigantic young fellow, once more seizing the unfortunate mealmonger by the throat, when out again went his tongue, like a piece of machinery touched by a spring, and again were the red eyes, now almost starting out of his head, turned round, whilst he himself was in a state of suffocation, that rendered his appearance ludicrous beyond description; 'it's a lie, I say, for you have neither thruth nor heart – that's what we all know.'

Now, we deny Brian's position that 'every mealmonger is a curse and a scourge to the country'; and we furthermore add that this prejudice, which Mr. Carleton has exerted himself to foster, is the most grievous aggravation of the calamities of Irish famine. A cry is raised against the exorbitant profit obtained by merchants on the import of corn, and Government is asked to intervene; but common sense tells us that the higher these profits are the more will persons engage in the trade – and, consequently, the more food will be imported into the country. To cut down those profits would be to cut down the trade, to diminish the imports and to aggravate the famine. Similar results attend the raising of a cry against corn-dealers and millers – which we are sorry to see encouraged by those who should know better. But worse than all is the clamour against the petty retailers: for in 1822 it was found to have created a sad impediment to the distribution of food in the villages and country-places after cargoes of provision had reached the harbours. Men will not undertake the retailing of corn when the principle of the trade is declared to be that 'they must buy and sell, and live by the loss', – much less when some furious Brian is taught that to strangle them is meritorious. It is an easy thing to plunder bakers' shops and meal stores; but where this becomes a practice there will soon be neither shops nor stores to be plundered – and every alleviation of famine will thus be rendered all but impossible. Bad as Skinadre may be, he saves the peasants from a journey of many miles to purchase food. The 'Panorama of Misery' in the retailer's shop would have made room for a far worse exhibition if the shop had been closed or destroyed.

Mr Carleton has more justly and truthfully described another class of persons, – a class that in every season of Irish distress has fearfully aggravated the evil and increased the difficulty of applying a remedy:–

The cry of the people was for either bread or work; and to still, if possible, this woeful clamour, local committees, by large subscriptions, aided, in some cases, by loans from government, contrived to find them employment on useful public works. Previous to this nothing could surpass the prostration and abject subserviency with which the miserable crowds solicited food or labour. Only give them labour at any rate – say sixpence a day – and they do not wish to beg or violate the laws. No, no; only give them peaceful employment, and they would rest not only perfectly contented, but deeply grateful. In the mean time, the employment they sought for was provided, not at sixpence, but at one-and-sixpence a day; so that for a time they appeared to feel satisfied, and matters went on peaceably enough. This, however, was too good to last. There are ever, amongst such masses of people, unprincipled knaves, known as 'politicians' – idle vagabonds, who hate all honest employment themselves, and ask no better than to mislead and fleece the ignorant and unreflecting people, however or whenever they can. These fellows read and expound the papers on Sundays and holidays; rail not only against every government, no matter what its principles are, but, in general, attack all constituted authority, without feeling one single spark of true national principle, or independent love of liberty. It is such corrupt scoundrels that always assail the executive of the country, and at the same time supply the official staff of spies and informers with their blackest perjurers and traitors. In truth, they are always the first to corrupt, and the first to betray. You may hear these men denouncing government this week, and see them strutting about the Castle, its pampered instruments, and insolent with its patronage, the next. If there be a strike, conspiracy, or cabal of any kind, these 'patriots' are at the bottom of it; and wherever ribbonism and other secret societies do *not* exist, *there* they are certain to set them a-going.

This mischievous class, so faithfully described in the passage just quoted, would not possess the influence they do if persons of higher station did not to a dangerous extent sanction the delusions which they propagate. Mr Carleton himself joins in the preposterous cry against forestallers, over-holders and keepers of corn-stores. We cannot allow even a tale to give currency to fallacies which demonstrably increase the calamities of Irish famine. Mr Carleton has deserved too much of his country – and even in this little work has manifested too much of power and generous feeling – for us to censure his errors with anything like bitterness or severity; but we grieve to find that he has been involved in the general torrent of delusion which has swept away all the boundaries of moderation and common sense, which has perilled the means of present safety and raised impediments in the way of future improvement.

The Earl of Rosse's[2] 'Letters on the State of Ireland' dwell at length on a subject to which Mr Carleton has alluded in his tale – the tenure of land in Ireland. If some malignant being had contrived a scheme so mutually injurious to landlord and tenant as that which has grown up in Ireland, we might, with the ancient Persians, believe in the reign of Ahriman.[3] The absurd tenancy of lives renewable for ever – the sub-division of land – the increase of the population beyond the existing means of employment – the perplexing questions of occupancy – and many other social evils are exposed by Lord Rosse: but we doubt whether an increase of the landlord's power of ejectment would remedy the evil, – even if it were accompanied by large facilities for emigration.

Our reasons for dissenting from Lord Rosse's proposition will be found in the last chapter of Mr G. L. Smyth's work; – which contains a sad history of the legislation connected with the land in Ireland. This, however, is a subject too extensive to be usefully discussed in a literary periodical; and we must, therefore, content ourselves with referring those who feel an interest in the subject to Mr Smyth's very accurate and careful compilation.

APPENDIX II

Athenaeum, 813 (30 September 1843), pp. 878–80
REPEAL SONGS OF MUNSTER
Songs, Ballads, and Skellig Lists. Cork, Hely.
The Spirit of the Nation. Dublin, Duffy.

SEVEN years have elapsed [*Ath.* No. 472] since we introduced the Munster Melodies to our readers as specimens of 'a new school of poetry, a new system of civilization, an original code of laws, and a language so purely native that it has not yet submitted to the fetters of grammar.' The Munster Muses have not been idle during this interval, but unfortunately they have changed the character of their strains; they have become controversialists and politicians, staunch advocates of Romanism and Repeal, claimants to the gift of prophecy, and not unfrequently garnishing their predictions with bits of personal satire. There are those who attribute this change to the influence of the Kildare Street Society's schools: they tell us that the Catholic scholars being compelled to conform so far to Protestant rule as to read the Scriptures daily, regarded this requisition as a tax imposed upon education, a badge of inferiority maintained in the spirit of ascendancy, and a mode of effecting that proselytism which the Society publicly disavowed; and that bitterness and personality first began to manifest themselves in the Munster Melodies just as the generation trained in the Kildare Street schools began to take an active part on the busy stage of life; and certain it is that ballad-controversy has largely increased wherever attempts have been made to set aside the national system of education in order to establish schools on more exclusive principles. A new generation, trained chiefly in the national schools, is just beginning to appear in public life; its most striking peculiarity is, that it is more purely English in language and habits of thought than the Anglo-Irish themselves. In localities where nothing but Gaelic was spoken some years ago, it is now exceedingly rare to find any one between the ages of twelve and twenty-five who does not speak English, and who does not use that language in preference, because it is the language in which he has learned to think. Even in remote rural districts, it is commonly said that Irish has become as rare as English was some twenty years ago. The change in this respect is confirmed by the testimony of the ballad-vendors; they say that there is now scarcely any sale for the ballads written in native Irish, and exhibit the assortments which they furnish to itinerant retailers for fairs and markets, in proof that the English language is fast establishing itself in every part of the country.

This little work which we have named at the head of the article appears a very fair exponent of the literary taste of the generation entering upon life, while the Repeal songs and controversial ballads of the broad sheet, furnish at least as accurate an index to the taste of the generation by which the busy stage is at present occupied. Thus viewed, the contrast between them appears striking. We say nothing respecting the political or religious character of these songs, but looking mainly to their moral and intellectual bearing, it is impossible not to see that the older ballads exhibit a vagueness of idea, and recklessness of expression, that characterize men wanting something, but not exactly knowing what, while the songs of *The Nation*, which are universally popular with the youth of Ireland, and indeed almost exclusively the poetry read by all between the ages of sixteen and twenty, display an earnestness and vehemence, with occasional bursts of fiery energy, which could only result from fixed and determinate resolution.

The first ballad to which we shall draw attention includes a prophecy which is to have its fulfilment in the present year, and is entitled 'The Distressed Maid of Erin!' Its style belongs to the old school of Munster Melodies, when candidates for the office of hedge-school-master were compelled to recite some ballad of their own composition as a proof of their qualifications. On these occasions it was their custom to use words 'of learned length and thundering sound', with very little attention to their meaning or appropriateness, and to adorn the verse with classical allusions of the most recondite nature, so as to amaze the rustics with the profundity of their learning. O'Healy, the author of the following song, is one of the last survivors of this school; he unites in his person the qualifications of mathematical teacher, village bard, and land-surveyor:

> You Nine sublime, receive my petition,
> Pity my condition, and raise my ambition
> With a few scrolls those lines to compose,
> So I now ardently implore your assistance,
> To inspire me with a flow of eloquence,
> All in consequence of a droll song I mean for to compose.
> Touching and tracing a fair maid's brilliancy,
> Who interrogated the state of my country,
> And that has bewildered my dreams incessantly,
> Lulled on a couch in sweet repose.
>
> This immaculate creature had sure astonished me,
> Embower'd by God's decree beneath an aspen tree,
> On a seat sedate, in majestic state,
> The mother of Cupid I thought her for to be;
> But she soon attracted me up to vanity,
> And in a strange heat my heart did beat;

Had I by chance the place of residence
Of Lord Doneraile or Hely Hutchinson,
I'd sell them by mortgage and all by articles,
To chase a hare on her golden estate.

Could I but cope with Homer's eloquence,
To each distant settlement, fearing no detriment,
Her mode in prose I'd quickly transpose;
Then Hector and Jason would fawn on her personage,
So would Achilles vie with Hercules,
In rowing ashore my love to export;
Those champions would fight with great animosity,
The bravest by right to enjoy her majesty,
The valleys with harmony echoing equally,
Each home stroke with a sounding report.

This prolific dale I ranged for curiosity,
With civil authority and kind urbanity,
Saying hail! my wandering maid,
And suffer'd no great delay in her perplexity,
But now her dexterity cheats my fidelity,
Her native state, profession and trade;
Are you the Parnassian part of the family,
Who through ancient wars exchanged her lenity,
And caused such calamity drowned in eternity,
By her regression of aid in Babylon's shade?

Or are you the lightsome Dido or Proserpine,
Or the Queen who voluntarily did accompany
And was decoyed by Paris to Troy,
And left many a list to muster her energy,
Deranged by jealousy in passing soliloquy,

Trying once more his rights to enjoy?
If you be a sporting roving frolicker,
From Paphos' grove, for the use of foreigners,
With kind hospitality and officious philanthropy
I'll supply you with blisses of joy.

Bless me, O'Healy, your tedious inquisition,
In a composition, would pierce the disposition
Of the wild and wise of the feminine kind,
It makes me deny to be Dido or Proserpine,
Or the Grecian consort, who most unfortunately
Despised and left her husband behind;
In the annals of fame my name is inserted free,
Tho' big-bellied bears had thought to convert me,
For James had neglected, and William subjected me
Alongside the Boyne, where I was confined.

Indeed, sir, I'm a maid that's weak and languid,
A sighing young damsel that's teased by fanatics,
My bones are broke – I'm tormented full sore;
The year twenty-nine had partly vanquished;
The doings of Calvin were then examined,
And be it known from the poet of sweet Donoughmore
That the year forty-three will end all our agony,
As St John the Divine has divined in his prophecy,
From that year out, no more animosity-
And so forth – there's an end to my scroll.

Another prophetical song is entitled 'A Dialogue with the Ruins of an Old Monastery'. It is not destitute of literary merit; though the rhymes are frequently rugged and imperfect, there is an harmonious flow in the run of the verse. Some of the sentiments are borrowed from Ward's Hudibrastic History of the Reformation, of which several cheap editions have been published in Dublin, and have proved very good speculations.

> In the year twenty-four I took a short tour
> On the beautiful shore of Old Erin,
> To view her dear plains and her clear winding streams,
> Which Providence framed so ensnaring;
> The nightingale nice with his harmonious voice,
> Made Nature rejoice in each station;
> This enchanting scene on our island so green
> Made me surely esteem Paddy's nation.
>
> For a churchyard was near, then my course I did steer
> Where a few silent tears I vented:
> To see the sad state of those buildings so great,
> Their awful defeat I lamented.
> When I thought on that clan that invaded our land,
> Whose impious hands caused vexation,
> And strove by all means like the cursed ancient Danes
> To gall the true remains of our nation.
>
> Quite silent I mused, my mind being confused,
> To behold the abused holy temple,
> All wrecked and defaced by a profligate race,
> That on virtue and grace long have trampled;
> My heart it did bleed on beholding the weeds
> Spring up where good deeds once were stationed,
> And the ivy, alas, all hung round where the mass
> Had been read to each class in our nation.

Said I, noble pile, then who did you defile?
Or why are you spoiled or deformed?
Or what wicked crime have you done in your time,
That here you're declined, mocked and scorned?
Now answer me sure, have you been impure,
Or loaded the poor with taxation,
Or tore life or land from the creature called man,
Thus bewildered to stand in our nation?

In low solemn strains spoke the holy remains,
With language quite plain and sincere then,
Now since it is so that you would wish to know
The cause of my woe, I'll declare then:
A licentious knave, that is now in his grave,
Old Harry, a slave to temptation,
My altars profaned and my ornaments gleaned,
And my clergymen slain thro' the nation.

But tell me, I pray, what caused him to stray,
That once did obey and respect you?
Was he not your friend, and your faith defend,
When Luther, the fiend, did reject you?
He stood for your cause, your maxims and laws,
Which gained him applause in his station.
Can it be the case that he acted so base,
For to bring disgrace on the nation?

Kind sir, it appears, that when he lived near
To twenty long years with his wife, sir,
He got quite enchanted with a comely young dame,
Which was the sole means of his strife, sir;

To Rome he applied but his suit being denied,
He then stepped aside from salvation,
And barbarously slew every person he knew,
That to popery was true in the nation.

Your words strike a dart thro' my poor sinful heart,
Which makes me to smart in great torment,
Because that each man didn't rise thro' the land,
For no human hand should lie dormant,
And all gather round this domestic clown,
And straight pull him down with impatience,
That left you forlorn, all split, wrecked and torn,
That once did adorn our nation.

My dear worthy sir, to attempt for to stir,
Would only incur the displeasure
Of our Saviour dear, who was mocked, scoffed and jeered,
And flogged most severe beyond measure;
When nailed to a cross without any remorse,
By merely the dross of creation,
His Father he called for to pardon their fall,
A lesson for all through each nation.

That structure then said, My friend, don't be dismay'd,
The church that Christ made will reign victor,
Hell's gates can't prevail, tho' they do her assail,
Pursue well my tale in the scripture.
St. Matthew explore the fifth chapter o'er,
The 18th verse in its station,
Will prove that she'll shine to the last day of time
Both pure and divine thro' the nation.

Another specimen of prophetic controversy is an imaginary dialogue between a handsome new Roman Catholic chapel, now in process of erection, and its neighbour, old Shandon church. This chapel is one of the lions of Cork; it was projected by Father Mathew, and all the subscriptions were collected by his individual exertions:–

A Discussion between a Church and a Chapel.

One morning early, as day was breaking,
Being in the charming sweet month of May,
When Flora's mantle had decorated
The fragrant plains all in rich array;
The lofty mountains I could survey them,
The purling streams and the river clear–
The crystal fountains and billows rolling,
Where ships were sailing from far and near.

I being reconciled with the sweets of nature,
I was preparing to take my way,
Till overhearing a conversation
A while occasioned me to stay;
Being a discussion in that place had taken,
Between new neighbours, near to Cork town,
About the chapel founded by Father Mathew;
But Shandon Church it began to frown.

This Church it broke out from its silence,
And in great violence to the Chapel said,
What spark are you that stand behind me?
My friends and neighbours you have betrayed,
My predecessors you did inveigle,
To renegade from their native home,
Where my ancestors are clad in earth,
And are still remaining 'till the day of doom.

The prudent Chapel soon made answer,
And was not angry, nor yet confused;
Madame, sitting in your pomp and grandeur,
I beg the favour to be excused;
Tho' here I'm standing both poor and naked,
I do inveigle nor flatter none–
I was erected by true Milesians–
My ordination is the Church of Rome.

Don't you remember, in former ages,
When you were naked as well as me?
Till by Church cess you did invade us,
Oppressing creatures with tyranny;
The tithes and taxes that you were craving,
We freely give you, tho' not your due;
They did belong to the Priests and Jesuits,
Whose ordination from Christ was true.

The holy Temple begun by David,
Was bare and naked awhile, like me,
Till by King Solomon it was supported,
A house of prayer and great dignity;
It was Christ began my first foundation,
To the end of days I will firm stand,
And with open arms I will receive
All Adam's race with the cross in hand.

The holy Scripture it clearly shows us,
The wicked forces of heresy
By King Pharaoh were then supported,
To the law of Moses would not agree,

Till with a plague they were afflicted
With snakes and serpents throughout the land;
The Israelites they were pursuing,
The sea consumed them by God's command.

The tithes and taxes will be defeated
And the Proctor's race will soon stand still;
The three hundred years the Serpent gave them,
Are clearly traced now by Columbkill;
When you are a shelter for owls and ravens
To perforate and reduce your walls,
Then I will flourish each morning gaily,
With joy-bells echoing, my flocks to call.

The first beginning of this new Chapel
Was in eighteen hundred and thirty-three;
It will soon be finished by the subscribers,
And all those tyrants then must flee;
There pious Christians will flock in numbers,
To heal their souls at this blessed ground,
To have the benefit of the Christian prayers,
Till the Judgment day, when the trumpets sound.

To bring those verses to a conclusion,
I won't intrude on the Muses nine;
Good Christians all that now peruse them,
I hope you'll excuse my stupid mind.
One request I am earnest craving,
The fervent prayers of both old and young,
For my assistance to gain salvation,
And all true members of the Church of Rome.

Turning from the controversial to the purely political songs, we find it no easy matter to select the most illustrative from the pile before us. Perhaps, after all, popularity is the safest guide; and we shall give precedence to that which has gone through an unparalleled number of editions, during the few months that have elapsed since its publication.

Erin go Bragh.
Air –'Exile of Erin'.

Once more pray assist me, ye bards of those ages
Who stroll round Parnassus and thirst for renown;
Assist me, ye Muses, ye Graces, and sages,
In those simple verses I'm going to pen down.
Then, then, to the subject, to me so endearing,
I fling forth my weak simple talents and a',
In praise of my country, my green mantled Erin,
The land of O'Connell, Erin go bragh.

O! Erin, my country, thou land of great splendour,
The relics of greatness are seen through thy plains,
O witness the ruins of thy buildings and grandeur,
And think on the time of great Brian and the Danes.
Yes, yes, thou'rt the land of Burke, Sheridan and Grattan,
Great Sarsfield, Moore, Curran, and Mathew, agra,
And holy St. Patrick, whose name is so pat in
The hearts of the offspring of Erin go bragh.

Then why should we be dragged thro' each mire and channel,
By proud, haughty Britain – have we no resource?
Yes, yes, we've our, leader, immortal O'Connell,
And to none we're inferior in physical force;

A teetotaller's a man that was ne'er beat in battle,
He could handle the gun, and the sword he could draw,
And tho' bullets should whistle, and cannons should rattle,
He'd be true to the cause of old Erin go bragh.

Tho' the Tories of England with vile names may taunt us,
And call us a rabble, and our priests ruffians vile,
Yet the time it will come when they surely will want us,
And then they must give us our own little isle.
For in spite of John Bull, then fair Freedom's unfurl'd,
We're backed by our friends, tho' they are far awa';
And the theme of the freemen, all over the world–
O'Connell, Repeal, and sweet Erin go Bragh.

Then rouse you, Milesians, arouse from your slumber,
And lash to the helm the ranks of Repeal;
Arouse you, Teetotallers, six millions in number,
Since liberty's wafted along on the gale.
Oh! where is the Irishman who'd be unwilling,
When to him the famed Repeal warden should ca'
To spare for his country one small annual shilling,
To carry Repeal for sweet Erin go bragh?

So now, as I mean to make a conclusion,
Long life and success to our virtuous Queen;
May her reign be in peace, without any confusion,
For she's well disposed towards the island of green.
Put an end to all strife, and away with disunion,
And let all your actions be inside the law,
And let your watch-word be Repeal of the Union,
O'Connell, brave Grattan, and Erin go bragh.

Another song, to the popular air of Ballinamona Oro, takes up the cause of the dismissed magistrates, in the following strain:–

> Honour and glory to you, my Lord Ffrench,[1]
> On the Irish Woolsack will soon be your bench,
> Then a fig for that despot – a disgrace to the wig;
> O his name it would shame poor Nell Flaherty's pig.
> Singing Ballinamona Oro,
> Ballinamona Oro,
> Ballinamona Oro,
> Repeal and O'Connell for me.
>
> There's another old wizard, he is playing a trick;
> Too proud to reign, so poor fellow took sick;
> Such intricate jokers the world never saw:
> They disappointed poor Roden, and they bother'd poor Shaw.[2]
> Singing, &c.
>
> Now for Booby Bernard,[3] a rogue or a fool,
> From the hot-bed of faction – the old Brandon [*sic*] School –
> He was like one overtaken by thunder and hail,
> When trumpet-tongued Bandon it shouted Repeal.
> Singing, &c.

The poor bard concludes with an allusion to the mishap of one of his brethren, and at the same time assigns a curious cause of confidence in his own escape from similar misfortune:–

> O yet, with all our vaunting, 'tis strange for to tell,
> A ballad-singer last week was confined in Clonmel,
> But my song I will sing, and I fear no fellow's frown,
> We have now Repeal Lawyers in every town.
> Singing, &c.

Every repeal demonstration and monster meeting has been duly chronicled in song; that of Tara Hill has been the most celebrated, as might have been expected, from the associations of the locality with the history of Ireland, previous to the Anglo-Norman invasion. The following is the best of the score devoted to celebrating this display:–

> Draw near, you Irish hearts of oak,
> You brave old Tara heroes,
> The chain that binds us must be broke,
> In spite of all those Neroes.
> O'Connell gives you great applause
> Throughout this Irish nation;
> You're foremost in Hibernia's cause,
> In quest of liberation.
>
> *Chorus*
> Hurra for Dan and noble Steel,
> The pride of Erin's nation:
> In spite of Wellington or Peel,
> We'll gain our liberation.
>
> On Tara's hill, the other day,
> Five hundred thousand did assemble;
> Teetotallers did sweetly play,
> Our foes for to make tremble;
> The road were neatly arched with green,
> Our flags hoisted in rotation,
> Three cheers were given for the Queen,
> And four for liberation.

When gallant Dan to Tara came,
Our boys did bravely cheer him,
He roused the hearts of old and young,
That assembled there to hear him.
He'll surely free us from the yoke,
If our aid we freely lend him;
You would think it was an angel spoke,
For the Clergy did attend him.

Think on the words of noble Steel,
Of the Protestant communion;
To our enemies he'll never yield,
Until we repeal the Union.
He tells us if we all unite,
In spite of all alarms,
We'll surely gain the glorious fight,
Without the force of arms.

Kilkenny, Cork, and Limerick too,
Call for the rights of Granua;
Tipperary showed what they could do,
In Cashel and in Nenagh;
Five hundred thousand on the plains,
Demanding liberation.
Not half that number swept the Danes
Far from our Irish nation.

God bless our Queen – long may she reign;
What foe dare to offend her?
Granua's sons with swords and guns
Are ready to defend her;

Long live each man that joins with Dan–
No matter what communion;
But in spite of all the Tory clan,
He will repeal the Union.[4]

Passing over the songs recording O'Connell's progress, though sorely tempted to quote that which describes his triumphal entry into Cork, we turn to one of a different character, which is not less popular within the sound of the bells of Bow, than it is amongst those who listen to the bells of Shandon:–

The Poor Irish Stranger in London.

O pity the fate of a poor Irish stranger,
That wandered thus far from his home,
I sigh for protection from want, woe and danger,
But I know not which way for to roam;
I ne'er shall return to Hibernia's green bowers,
Where tyranny has trampled the sweetest of flowers;
They gave comfort to me in my loneliest hours,
But they are gone – I shall ne'er see them more.

With wonder I gazed on the high lofty mountain,
As in grandeur it rose from its lord,
And with sorrow beheld my own garden yielding
The choicest of fruits for its board;
But where is my father's low cottage of clay,
Where I've spent many a long happy day,
Alas! has his lordship contrived it away?
Yes, 'tis gone – I shall ne'er see it more.

When the sloe and the berry hung ripe on the bushes,
I have gathered them off without harm,
And I've gone to the fields where I've shorn the green rushes,
Preparing for winter's cold storm;
I have sat by the fire of a cold winter's night,
Along with my friends, telling tales of delight;
Those days gave me pleasure, and I could invite–
But they're gone – I shall ne'er see them more.

O Erin, sad Erin, it grieves me to ponder
The wrongs of thy injured isle;
Thy sons, many thousands, deploring do wander
On shores far away, in exile.
But give me the power to cross over the main,
America might yield me some shelter from pain,
I'm only lamenting while here I remain,
For the joys I shall never see more.

Farewell then to Erin, and all those left weeping
Upon thy disconsolate shore;
Farewell to the grave where my father lies sleeping,
That ground I will ever adore.
Farewell to each pleasure – I once had a home,
Farewell, now a stranger in England I roam;
Oh give me my freedom, or give me my tomb,
Yes, in pity – I'll ask for no more.

The world has borne testimony to the wisdom of the statesman who preferred the power of making a nation's ballads to that of making a nation's laws; we have given specimens of the ballads which, from their extensive circulation, appear to be the exponents of popular feeling in the south of Ireland. From the way in which most of them refer to the repeal of the Union, it appears that they have no very definite idea of the real nature and effects of such a measure; they seem to regard it as a mysterious something by which their grievances will be redressed, and the elements of prosperity in the country developed for the benefit of its inhabitants. This is sufficiently manifest in the following stanzas:

> We have noble members to stand to our cause,
> To obtain for Granua her just rights and laws;
> Keep sober and steady, and then I go bail
> That Dan gets for Ireland a speedy Repeal.
>
> That trade it may flourish in Ireland once more,
> We'll have peace and plenty as we had before;
> Each man for his labour well paid he must be,
> So we'll live in contentment in Erin ma chree.

From these ballads it is also evident that the cry of Repeal has been taken up, not so much for its own sake as because it has been recommended by the leader; praises of O'Connell are more numerous and more hearty than aspirations for Repeal. To such an extent is vagueness of object combined with strong personal attachment to the leader, that in one song the highest praise given to the Goddess of freedom is that 'she is like O'Connell's daughter'; and in another the popular demands are said to consist of 'the rights he showed we wanted'. It deserves to be further remarked, that many of the old symbolic songs in which the Jacobites of the last century professed their secret allegiance to the Pretender have been modernized and applied to O'Connell. He figures as 'the blackbird' – 'the green linnet' – 'the white horse' – 'Daniel in the lion's den' – 'Moses' – 'the hope of Erin' – and, whimsically enough, as 'the grey mare', an animal said to have been ridden very roughly by successive generations, but which is now on the point of throwing its rider. The promised publication of the Jacobite relics of Ireland will probably afford us an opportunity of showing how the same symbols have been applied to different leaders of opposition or revolt for three centuries; but at present we shall quote only one symbolic ballad, in which O'Connell appears as the White Rose of Tara's bower. It may be interesting to remark, that the Irish, in the wars of the Roses, were zealous supporters of the House of York, and that the white rose has been the favourite cognizance of Irish insurgents ever since the days of Lambert Simnel and Perkin Warbeck.[5]

You true sons of Erin, be faithful and steady,
And to your Queen most royal be loyal and ready,
To come to the bower with full powers just and legal;
It was on Mount St. Jean[6] where we cleared off the eagle.

Chorus.
Will you, will you, will you, will you
Come to the bower?

Will you come to the bower where my flower I have planted?
For Cork County he's elected, with courage most undaunted.
I will show a sight most delightful and pleasing,
Unto all honest hearts of every persuasion.

Will you come to the bower, where my flower it is blooming,
And a most stately air of late is assuming?
It blooms in Merrion-square,[7] and a native is of Kerry,
It is esteemed at Kildare and at Wexford Ferry.

Will you come to the bower, where my flower it blooms daily,
With a shamrock so green and a sprig of shillelagh?
All over Paddy's land its branches are extending,
Though under state squalls and storms it was bending.

Will you come to the bower, towards royal Tamar,
Where we planted our rights in spite of each defamer?
Around Tara's Hall we will call our fine heroes,
The true sons of O'Neill and the brave Glanville heroes.

Will you come to the bower, where my flower is in blossom?
And Lord Sarsfield of old he wore it in his bosom.
By a blast from the Hague it lay fading and dying,
But now with the White Rose once more is reviving.

Will you come to the bower, and my flower's name I'll tell it?
With a D. and an O'C. most nobly you can spell it.
I'll send it in a barge over St. George's deep channel,
It is blooming in the house – my flower is O'Connell.

Will you come to the bower, where my flower will take root in?
And the harp it shall play to the air of Lord Lucan;[8]
Our Queen is of the race of old famed Caledonia,
But Daniel is our jewel, and a true Anemona.

When seated in the bower, if Peel, Wellington, or others
Dare to oppose him, we will go off like brothers;
And on Mount St. Jean once more pluck the lily,
As we have now obtained what we lost by Orange Billy.

Chorus.

The specimens we have extracted, sufficiently illustrate the character of the Repeal Songs of the older school; the lyrics of the New academy must next claim our attention, and they are sufficiently important to require an article for themselves.

Athenaeum 832 (7 October 1843) pp. 899–900.
The Spirit of the Nation
[Second Notice.]

ACCORDING to our promise, we now turn to the new and rising school of poetry, which, as we said in our article on Repeal Songs last week, is chiefly patronised by the generation just beginning to take a part in active life. The lyrics of this new school are published in a paper recently established in Dublin, called *The Nation*; a paper bearing the most obvious marks of being chiefly conducted by young men; its articles are full of spirit and temper, but are not equally remarkable for temper and discretion; its most powerful appeals are made to the passions rather than the judgment, and its high tone of self-reliance sometimes assumes the form of that overweening confidence, not to say presumption, which is so often found to be a drawback on youthful cleverness. The songs published in this paper display considerable beauty, both of language and imagery, combined with intense feeling. The best pieces in the collection have fictitious signatures attached to them, intimating that the writers are natives of Munster, and this circumstance greatly increases the effect of the contrast between the new and old schools of Munster poetry. The new school leaves no room for mistaking the objects of its advocacy; no one can misapprehend the very first song in the collection:–

The work that should to–day be wrought
Defer not till to-morrow;
The help that should within be sought,
Scorn from without to borrow.
Old maxims these – yet stout and true –
They speak in trumpet tone,
To do at once what is to do,
And trust ourselves alone.

Too long our Irish hearts we schooled,
In patient hope to bide;
By dreams of English justice fooled,
And English tongues that lied.
That hour of weak delusion's past,
The empty dream has flown:
Our hope and strength, we find at last,
Is in ourselves alone.

Aye! bitter hate, or cold neglect,
Or lukewarm love, at best,
Is all we've found or can expect,
We aliens of the west.
No friend, beyond her own green shore,
Can Erin truly own,
Yet stronger is her trust, therefore,
In her brave sons alone.

* * * *

The 'foolish word impossible'
At once, for aye disdain;
No power can bar a people's will
A people's right to gain.

> Be bold, united, firmly set,
> Nor flinch in word or tone–
> We'll be a glorious nation yet,
> Redeemed – erect – alone.[9]

In the older ballads of Munster the allusions to oppressive exercise of a landlord's rights are faint and timid; but the *Nation* knows neither fear nor scruple in denouncing those whom it calls Exterminators; 'the Exterminator's Song' is one which has taken a strong hold in Ireland. We shall quote only the first verse:–

> 'Tis I am the poor man's scourge,
> And where is the scourge like me?
> My land from all Papists I purge,
> Who think that their votes should be free–
> Who think that their votes should be free!
> From huts only fitted for brutes,
> My agent the last penny wrings;
> And my serfs live on water and roots,
> While I feast on the best of good things!
> For I am the poor man's scourge!
> For I am the poor man's scourge!
> (*Chorus* of the Editors of 'The Nation')
> Yes, *you* are the poor man's scourge!
> But of *such* the whole island we'll purge!

There is but little adulation of O'Connell in these songs, and some opinions which he is known to entertain are not treated with much respect or ceremony. For instance, O'Connell speaks slightingly of the United Irishmen, and he believes that their premature agitation was a principal cause of all the evils which Ireland endured at the close of the last century. We need not enter into any discussion of a subject so full of pain and peril, but we shall quote a spirited song, which proves that a want of sympathy with the United Irishmen cannot be attributed to the conductors of the *Nation*:–

Who fears to speak of Ninety-eight?
Who blushes at the name?
When cowards mock the patriot's fate,
Who hangs his head for shame?
He's all a knave, or half a slave,
Who slights his country thus;
But a *true* man, like you, man,
Will fill your glass with us.

We drink the memory of the brave,
The faithful and the few –
Some lie far off beyond the wave,
Some sleep in Ireland, too;
All – all are gone – but still live on
The fame of those who died;
All true men, like you, men,
Remember them with pride.

Some on the shores of distant lands
Their weary hearts have laid,
And by the stranger's heedless hands
Their lonely graves were made,
But, though their clay be far away
Beyond the Atlantic foam –
In true men, like you, men,
Their spirit's still at home.

The dust of some is Irish earth;
Among their own they rest;
And that same land that gave them birth
Has caught them to her breast;
And we will pray that from that clay
Full many a race may start
Of true men, like you, men,
To act as brave a part.

They rose in dark and evil days
To right their native land;
They kindled here a living blaze
That nothing shall withstand,
Alas! that Might can vanquish Right –
They fell and pass'd away;
But true men, like you, men,
Are plenty here to-day.

Then here's their memory – may it be
For us a guiding light,
To cheer our strife for liberty,
And teach us to unite.
Through good or ill, be Ireland's still,
Though sad as theirs your fate;
And true men, be you, men,
Like those of Ninety-eight.[10]

A few of the *Nation's* songs have no connexion with politics, and these are among the best in the collection. There is a spirit of melancholy music in a wild irregular melody, which bears the title of 'My Grave':–[11]

Shall they bury me in the deep,
Where wind-forgetting waters sleep?
Shall they dig a grave for me,
Under the green-wood tree?
Or on the wild heath,
Where the wilder breath
Of the storm doth blow?
Oh, no! Oh, no!

Shall they bury me in the Palace Tombs,
Or under the shade of Cathedral domes?
Sweet 'twere to lie in Italy's shore;
Yet not there – nor in Greece, though I love it more.
In the wolf or the vulture my grave shall I find?
Shall my ashes career on the world-seeing wind?
Shall they fling my corpse in the battle mound,
Where coffinless thousands lie under the ground? –
Just as they fall they are buried so –
Oh, no! Oh, no!

No! on an Irish green hill-side,
On an opening lawn – but not too wide;
For I love the drip of the wetted trees–
On me blow no gales, but a gentle breeze,
To freshen the turf; put no tombstone there,
But green sods deck'd with daisies fair.
Nor sods too deep; but so that the dew,
The matted grass-roots may trickle through–
Be my epitaph writ on my country's mind,
'He serv'd his country and lov'd his kind'.
Oh! 'twere merry unto the grave to go,
If one were sure to be buried so.

The author of these lines has contributed some of the most exciting of the war-songs to this volume; in one of them he directly offers his services as a volunteer:–

> Let Britain brag her motley rag;
> We'll lift The Green more proud and airy;–
> Be mine the lot to bear that flag,
> And head The Men of Tipperary.

> Though Britain boasts her British hosts,
> About them all right little care we;
> Give us to guard our native coasts
> The Matchless Men of Tipperary.

We prefer the unknown Celt in his character of Alcaeus, and would gladly see him abandon that of Tyrtaeus, which clearly is not his natural vocation.[12]

A little piece, bearing the signature Clericus,[13] will remind our readers of Bryant; the Irish, like the American poet, 'has touched the plaintive chords of memory, and waked an echo in every heart':–

> Ah! why should I recall them – the gay, the joyous years,
> Ere hope was cross'd or pleasure dimm'd by sorrow and by tears?
> Or why should memory love to trace youth's glad and sunlit way,
> When those who made its charms sweet are gathered to decay?
> The summer's sun shall come again to brighten hill and bower –
> The teeming earth its fragrance bring beneath the balmy shower;
> But all in vain will mem'ry strive, in vain we shed our tears-
> They're gone away and can't return – the friends of boyhood's years!

Ah! why then wake my sorrow, and bid me now count o'er
The vanished friends so dearly prized – the days to come no more–
The happy days of infancy, when no guile our bosoms new,
Nor reck'd we of the pleasures that with each hour flew?
'Tis all in vain to weep for them – the past a dream appears;
And where are they – the lov'd, the young, the friends of
    boyhood's years?

Go seek them in the cold church-yard – they long have stolen
    to rest;
But do not weep, for their young cheeks by woe were ne'er
    oppressed;
Life's sun for them in splendour set – no cloud came o'er the ray
That lit them from this gloomy world upon their joyous way.
No tears about their graves be shed – but sweetest flow'rs be flung–
The fittest off'ring thou canst make to hearts that perish young–
To hearts this world has not torn with racking hopes and fears;
For bless'd are they who pass away in boyhood's happy years!

We pass over many pieces of power and beauty which are one-
sided and inaccurate in their historical allusions. From time
immemorial the plea in such cases has been–

Adzooks! must one swear to the truth of a song?

but the case before us cannot fairly claim this privilege; each poet
affects to speak, not for himself, but for a nation, and his voice is
more likely to be heard if its tones be marked by candour and kindness, than if he indulges in exaggeration, menace, and defianc e.
We wonder that an obvious inconsistency has escaped the clever
writers of these songs; at the very moment that they are writing
what they choose to consider as anti-English strains, their language

is English, their imagery English, their metres English, and no small portion of their allusions and their tunes purely English. It would be no difficult matter to show that the writers of several of the songs before us have studied Milton, Shakspeare, and other English bards until they have become penetrated with their spirit, and though nationally Irish they are intellectually, as was said of Fox, 'all over English'. This consideration ought to have suggested many abatements of that exclusive nationality which marks these songs, and it involves lessons of forbearance which may be profitably developed by the guides of public opinion on both sides of St George's Channel.

Notes

NOTES TO INTRODUCTION

1 Except where otherwise stated this account is based on Taylor's entry in the *Dictionary of National Biography*; see also my entry on him in the forthcoming *Dictionary of Irish Biography*. Attributions of *Athenaeum* articles to Taylor are based on an incomplete online bibliography of *Athenaeum* contributors *www.soi.city.ac.uk/~asp/v2/contributors/ contributorfiles/ TAYLOR,WilliamCooke.html* (last accessed 21 January 2004) unless otherwise stated. Users should note this file has no entries for 1829–30, 1832, 1835–8, 1840 and 1844, and some biographical data is inaccurate. Desmond Keenan's books, *Ireland 1800–1850* (Philadelphia, 2001) and *The Grail of Catholic Emancipation, 1793–1829* (Philadelphia, 2002), which draw heavily on the Whig *Dublin Evening Post*, provide useful insights on the Whig view of O'Connell. Thanks to Paul Bew, Sean Connolly, Derval Fitzgerald, Alvin Jackson, Peter Gray and James McGuire.

2 William Cooke Taylor, *History of the Civil Wars of Ireland* (London, 1831), II, pp. 270–1; Samuel Hayman/W. G. Field, *Handbook for Youghal* (Youghal, 1896), p. 63 dates this takeover by Lord Shannon to 1744. Shannon's control of the borough was broken in the 1820s when the Whig Duke of Devonshire successfully used his foreshore rights to claim ownership of housing built on land reclaimed from the estuary (ibid., p. 81).

3 Taylor, *Civil Wars*, II, pp. 300–26; Hayman/Field, *Handbook*, pp. 75–8. [Hayman's grandfather was Mayor of Youghal in the 1790s, the town's leading loyalist.]

4 *Memoirs of William Sampson, an Irish exile, written by himself . . . With an introduction, detailing the causes of the Irish insurrection in 1798, and Notes, by the author of the History of the Civil Wars of Ireland* (London, 1832).

5 *Irish Book Lover*, Aug.–Sept. 1920, pp. 19–20.

6 Taylor, *Civil Wars*, II, pp. 327–30.

7 Ibid., p. 65.

8 Hayman/Field, *Handbook*, p. 55.

9 Taylor, *Civil Wars of Ireland*, II, p. 16n; W. C. Taylor (ed. and trans.), Gustave de Beaumont *Ireland: Social, Political, and Religious* (London, 1839) I, p. 121n. The date 1810 derives from Hayman/Field *Handbook* which states that restoration in that year made the church resemble 'a conventicle' (p. 23n).

10 Taylor (ed. and trans.), Beaumont, *Ireland*, II, 154n.

11 William Cooke Taylor *Romantic Biography of the Age of Elizabeth or Sketches of life from the Bye Ways of History* (London, 1842), p. viii.

12 D. H. Akenson, *A Protestant in Purgatory: Richard Whately, Archbishop of Dublin* (Hamden, Connecticut, 1981); Norman Vance, 'Improving Ireland: Richard Whately,

theology, and political economy' in Stefan Collini et al. (eds), *Economy: Polity and Society: British Intellectual History 1750–1950* (Cambridge, 2000), pp. 181–202; Thomas A. Boylan and Timothy Foley, *Political Economy and Colonial Ireland: The Propagation and Ideological Function of Economic Discourse in the Nineteenth Century* (London, 1992).

13 Taylor, *Romantic Biography of the Age of Elizabeth*, I, p. 5. Giovanni Pietro Caraffa (1476–1559), ascetic reformer and Inquisitor, was a leading collaborator of Pope Paul III (1534–49) in summoning the Council of Trent, and himself reigned unhappily as Pope Paul IV (1555–9); he refused to recognise the succession of Elizabeth I as Queen of England on the ground that she was illegitimate. Lorenzo Ganganelli (1705–74) as Pope Clement XIV (1769–74) suppressed the Jesuits.

14 Taylor reviews *Remains of Charles Dickinson* in *Athenaeum*, 2 Aug. 1845, pp. 757–8.

15 Donal Kerr, *Peel, Priests and People* (Oxford, 1983), pp. 293–5, 302.

16 Taylor, *Romantic Biography of the Age of Elizabeth*, I, p. 415.

17 Taylor *Civil Wars*, I, pp. 198, 243–6.

18 Ibid., I, p. 207.

19 Ibid., I, p. 153.

20 Ibid., II, p. 105.

21 Compare O'Connell's Belfast speech reported in William McComb, *The Repealer Repulsed* (new edn by Patrick Maume, Dublin, 2003; first published 1841), p. 74. Paul Bew has suggested to me that O'Connell may have derived the reference from his secretary, Taylor's fellow Blackwater Valley man W. J. O'Neill Daunt, who uses the same quotations for the same purpose in his *Ireland and her Agitators* (1857).

22 McComb, *Repealer Repulsed*, pp. 171, 223–4

23 E.g. *Athenaeum*, 2 Oct. 1841, p. 763 ('professors who comment on the Bible should first of all read it'); 3 July 1847, p. 701 (suggests medical treatment for the apocalyptic ravings of the Orange populist Rev. Tresham Gregg); 17 July 1847, p. 763 (an overenthusiastic Biblical commentator draws meanings from the English Bible which have no basis in the original Greek and Hebrew).

24 *Romantic Biography*, II, p. 159.

25 *Athenaeum*, 14 Feb. 1846, pp. 167–8.

26 William Cooke Taylor, *Notes of a Tour in the Manufacturing Districts of Lancashire: Letters to the Archbishop of Dublin* (London, 1842; 3rd edn, 1968).

27 Norman McCord, *The Anti-Corn Law League* (London, 1958), pp. 185–6; Paul A. Pickering and Alex Tyrrell, *The People's Bread: A History of the Anti-Corn Law League* (London, 2000), p. 43.

28 *Athenaeum*, 9 Jan. 1841 pp. 31–2.

29 *Athenaeum*, 25 Feb. 1843.

30 McCord, *Anti-Corn Law League*, pp. 143–4, 176.

31 Charles Gavan Duffy, *Thomas Davis* (London, 1890), pp. 304–5.

32 James Roderick O'Flanagan, *An Octogenarian Literary Life* (Cork, 1896), pp. 72–6; Hayman, *Handbook*, pp. 91–2.

33 Clarendon Papers, Bodleian Library, Oxford, Letterbook 1 (1847–8): Clarendon to Whately 3 August 1847; Clarendon to Russell 18 Oct. 1847; William Cooke Taylor, *Notes of*

a Visit to the Model Schools in Dublin, and Reflections on the state of the Education Question in Ireland, suggested by that visit (Dublin, 1847).

34 Clarendon Papers, Letterbook 1: Clarendon to Russell, 25 Aug. 1847.

35 Clarendon to Russell, 12 Oct. 1847; Clarendon to Cooke Taylor, 17 Oct. 1847.

36 Mary E. Daly, *The Spirit of Earnest Inquiry: The Statistical and Social Inquiry Society of Ireland* (Dublin, 1997).

37 Donal Kerr *'A Nation of Beggars': Priests, People and Politicians in Post-Famine Ireland* (Oxford, 1994), p. 150.

38 Thomas Pinney (ed.), *The Letters of Thomas Babington Macaulay* (Cambridge, 1981), V, pp. 66 [29 Aug. 1849], 86 [24 Dec. 1849; response to a letter asking him to chair a meeting to arrange support for Taylor's widow and family]. Taylor reviewed the first volumes of Macaulay's *History* in *Athenaeum*, leaving aside its Irish aspect for reviews of future volumes.

39 Thomas Carlyle, *Reminiscences of my Irish Journey in 1849* (London, 1882), pp. 43–5.

40 S. Shannon Millin, *The Statistical and Social Inquiry Society of Ireland: Historical Memoirs* (Dublin, 1920).

41 *Irish Book Lover*, June–July 1916, p. 182.

42 Justin C. Condon 'Literary worthies of Imokilly – additional notes', *Journal of the Cork Historical and Archaeological Society*, 1946, p. 86.

43 For example, the account of Robert Emmet recycles Taylor's review of the third series of R. R. Madden's *United Irishmen* (*Athenaeum* 12 Sept. 1846, pp. 930–2); it is clearly a warning to Young Ireland. The *Athenaeum* review of the first volume of O'Connell's *Life and Speeches* compiled by John O'Connell (2 May 1846, pp. 445–7) suspiciously resembles the account of O'Connell's early life and training in *Memoir*, even using the same quotations; the online *Athenaeum* contributor index does not ascribe it to Taylor, but this may be an oversight. (Taylor certainly reviewed the subsequent volume dealing with the Veto controversy – *Athenaeum* 9 Jan. 1847, pp. 40–1.)

44 Oliver MacDonagh, *O'Connell: The Life of Daniel O'Connell 1775–1847* (London, 1991), pp. 114, 122.

45 *Athenaeum*, 1 May 1847, pp. 459–60.

46 Oliver MacDonagh notes that O'Connell's later fervour reflected the baroque emotionalism of nineteenth-century devotional Catholicism rather than 'the simple, severe piety' of St Omer and Douai (*O'Connell*, p. 27).

47 Cf. Sean O Faolain, *King of the Beggars: A Life of Daniel O'Connell* (1938; new edn, Dublin, 1980), pp. 181–2.

48 *Athenaeum*, 28 Oct. 1843, pp. 960–2.

49 While O'Connell supported Free Trade, a minority view in agricultural Ireland, and supplied Repeal activists to defend League meetings in Britain against Chartist disruption, he made little effort to impose an unified anti-Corn Law line on his MPs; he was partly influenced by hope that the government might concede Repeal in order to concentrate on dealing with unrest in Britain; the anti-aristocratic worldview which he shared with the League leaders did not keep them from regarding him as irresponsible and untrust-worthy; the League never developed extensive organisation in Ireland, partly because

O'Connell did not wish to encourage a body outside his control. Pickering and Tyrrell, *The People's Bread*, pp. 41, 73–5, 81–3, 174.

50 Ibid., pp. 206–7; MacDonagh *O'Connell*, pp. 528–9.

51 Clarendon Papers, Letterbook 1: Clarendon to Russell, 16 July 1847

52 Charles Gavan Duffy, *Four Years of Irish History* (London, 1883), p. 204.

53 Christine Kinealy *The Great Irish Famine: Impact, Ideology and Rebellion* (Basingstoke, 2001).

54 Clarendon Papers, Letterbook 1: Clarendon to Russell, 12 Oct. 1847, to Cooke Taylor, 15 Oct. 1847, to Russell, 18 Oct. 1847.

55 Donal McCartney, *W. E. H. Lecky: Historian and Politician, 1838–1903* (Dublin, 1994).

56 *Athenaeum* 14 Feb. 1846, pp.167–8; Tom Hunt, *Portlaw, County Waterford 1825–76: Portrait of an Industrial Village and its Cotton Industry* (Maynooth, 2000).

57 Christopher Morash, *Writing the Irish Famine* (Oxford, 1995), pp. 157–8; Melissa Fegan, *Literature and the Irish Famine 1845–1919* (Oxford, 2002), pp. 148, 235, unaware of the author's identity, presents the review as 'an English viewpoint'.

58 K. D. M. Snell (ed.), Alexander Somerville, *Letters from Ireland during the Famine of 1847* (Dublin, 1994), pp. 174–5.

59 Pickering and Tyrrell, *The People's Bread*, p. 175.

60 Field/Hayman, *Handbook*, p. 94.

61 Robin Haines, *Charles Trevelyan and the Great Irish Famine* (Dublin, 2004), p. 53.

NOTES TO REMINISCENCES

1 In Sir Walter Scott's narrative poem, *The Lady of the Lake*.

2 This in fact influenced O'Connell away from conservatism and towards radicalism.

3 O'Connell joined the United Irishmen in 1797 while a member of the Lawyers' Corps (MacDonagh, *O'Connell*, pp. 54–7, 62–5).

4 Lord Wycombe, subsequently second Marquess of Lansdowne. Taylor was acquainted with his half-brother, the third Marquess, a Whig Cabinet minister to whom *Romantic Biography of the Age of Elizabeth* is dedicated.

5 (1750–1832) Leading English Catholic campaigner; a distinguished lawyer. The English Catholic committee, numerically weaker and more upper class than their Irish counterparts, tended to favour the veto (which they thought would increase their own influence over episcopal appointments).

6 The barrister William Saurin (1757–1839) had opposed the Union; his Huguenot ancestry with its memories of Catholic persecution made him a fierce opponent of Catholic Emancipation, and as Attorney-General for Ireland, 1807–22, he was regarded as the mainstay of the hardliners within the Dublin administration.

7 Although this was widely believed at the time, the article was in fact written by a Protestant member of the Catholic Board, John Finlay, Magee's senior counsel at the trial. (Denis Gwynn *Daniel O'Connell* (Cork, rev. edn, 1947) p. 98). O'Connell was, however, unintentionally responsible for the prosecution. The Prince Regent, infuriated by

O'Connell's speech on the 'witchery' resolutions, demanded that Peel should prosecute O'Connell; Peel decided this would be politically unwise but appeased the Regent by prosecuting Magee, who had published the speech. (Brian Inglis, 'O'Connell and the Irish Press 1800–42', *Irish Historical Studies* VIII, 29 (Mar. 1952), pp. 2–3.) Frederick William Conway (1777–1853), editor/proprietor of the *Evening Post*, 1814–43, with whom Taylor co-operated on Whig government propaganda, was profoundly influenced by the belief that O'Connell had not done enough for Magee after the editor's conviction. (Keenan, *Grail of Catholic Emancipation*, pp. 451–7).

8 This argument was used by the Duke of York in his 1826 House of Lords speech against that year's Catholic Relief Bill (Gwynn, *O'Connell*, pp. 158–9).

9 Gwynn, *O'Connell*, pp. 96–7 gives the context of this statement.

10 D'Esterre had been the only Alderman to oppose an anti-Emancipation resolution. He chose to treat O'Connell's reference to a 'beggarly' corporation as referring to D'Esterre's own precarious financial position.

11 On 31 January D'Esterre paraded along the quays to the Four Courts threatening to horsewhip O'Connell. He then took a stand at the corner of College Green, accompanied by several prominent Dublin Orangemen, in the hope of catching O'Connell as he returned home

12 Taylor has got his dates wrong. O'Connell's original statement was made on 21 January 1815; the duel took place on 1 February.

13 MacDonagh, *O'Connell*, pp. 137–8, 143; Gwynn, *O'Connell*, pp. 135–7. Amongst various gestures of penitence, O'Connell paid an annuity to one of D'Esterre's daughters and on one occasion travelled from Dublin to Cork to appear for Mrs. D'Esterre in a lawsuit without payment.

14 MacDonagh *O'Connell*, pp. 138–42; James Kelly, *'That Damn'd Thing Called Honour': Duelling in Ireland 1570–1860* (Cork, 1995), pp. 242–7.

15 Richard Hayes OFM, d.1824, based in Franciscan College, Wexford; well known in Ireland for preaching that the authors of Protestant Reformation were directly inspired by the Devil. His mission was complicated by the fact that he was an outspoken upholder of 'domestic nomination' the view that candidates for the Irish episcopacy should be nominated to Rome by the diocesan clergy rather than the bishops, and by the fact that the anti-vetoist position implied defiance of the Pope himself if he were to approve of the veto. Ercole Cardinal Consalvi (1757–1824) was Papal Secretary of State, and favourably disposed to the British government for diplomatic reasons; Lorenzo Cardinal Litta (1756–1820) was Prefect of the Roman Curia. Thomas Wyse (1791–1862), a Catholic landowner from Waterford, lived on the Continent for a decade, then played a leading role in the 1826 Waterford election; in 1829 published the major contemporary *History of the Catholic Association*. Whig MP for Tipperary 1830–2, for Waterford City 1835–47; junior Lord of the Treasury 1839–41. Opposed O'Connell's Repeal campaign; in 1843 joined Smith O'Brien in trying to show that Irish Whig MPs could make their presence felt at Westminster and represented a serious political alternative to O'Connellism. Strong supporter of the National Schools and Queen's Colleges. (J. J. Auchmuchty, *Sir Thomas Wyse* (London, 1939)). See also Keenan, *Grail of Catholic Emancipation*, pp. 259–60, 263–4, 275–6, 280, 286–8, 294–5.

16 This considerably underestimates O'Connell's literary interests; although the mistaken impression that O'Connell read only law books was very widespread, Taylor is also biased by a comparison with his own classic attainments and prolific historical writings.

17 *Memoir of Ireland, Native and Saxon* (1843). For Taylor's critical but slightly less contemptuous review, see *Athenaeum* 25 Feb. 1843. Taylor suggested O'Connell might have been better employed in writing an autobiography; the Tory *Dublin University Magazine* retorted that O'Connell's autobiography would probably have been as inaccurate as his history.

18 This letter, written by the Young Ireland priest Fr. John Kenyon of Templederry, appeared in the *Nation* shortly after O'Connell's death. It was widely reproduced by O'Connell's Old Ireland followers and caused considerable political damage to the Young Irelanders.

19 Henry Grattan junior, *Memoirs of the Life and Times of Henry Grattan* (5 vols, London, 1849: first published 1839–46) v, p. 536 records Grattan as commenting 'I am devoured by my own hounds'.

20 In the early 1830s.

21 James Warren Doyle (1786–1834), Catholic Bishop of Kildare and Leighlin 1819–34; a major reforming figure in the early nineteenth-century Irish Catholic Church and an ally of O'Connell in the Emancipation campaign. His outspoken writings on public and religious matters were signed J. K. L. [James Kildare and Leighlin] at a time when Catholic bishops rarely described themselves in public fora by the titles of their sees because only Church of Ireland bishops were formally recognised by the State; Doyle became generally known by the initials. As stated by Taylor, he favoured mixed education, and even put forward a plan for Anglican-Catholic reunion which considerably underestimated the doctrinal differences between the two churches; he also opposed Repeal.

22 John MacHale (1791–1881), Archbishop of Tuam 1834–81; made his name as a Maynooth professor in the 1820s with polemics against Evangelical anti-Catholicism; utterly opposed to the National Schools, which he regarded as a form of disguised proselytism. The most outspoken episcopal Repealer and leader of those bishops who opposed close co-operation with the state; known to his admirers as 'The Lion of the Fold of Judah'. Daniel Murray (1768–1852; archbishop of Dublin 1823–52), a significant episcopal reformer in the Dublin archdiocese, who pioneered many devotional innovations. Closely associated with O'Connell in Emancipation era, but lukewarm on Repeal; led the episcopal faction which favoured compromise with the state on education, and helped to deflate the Repeal campaign by willingness to accept legislative concessions from Peel. After O'Connell's death worked closely with Clarendon, who regarded him as a model bishop.

23 'The Irish Avatar' written by Byron in September 1821 denounces 'the fourth of the fools and oppressors called George IV', ridicules O'Connell and Lord Fingall as 'slaves, who now hail their betrayer with hymns', and contrasts their flunkeyism with 'the glory of Grattan, the genius of Moore'.

24 The bottle riot took place on 14 December 1822. The refusal to indict the prisoners was partly due to Wellesley's insistence that they should be charged with conspiracy to

murder him, rather than riotous behaviour (Fergus O'Ferrall, *Catholic Emancipation: Daniel O'Connell and the Birth of Irish Democracy 1820–30* (Dublin, 1985), pp. 13–14).

25 For Magee's role in intensifying religious conflict at this period, see Desmond Bowen, *The Protestant Crusade in Ireland 1800–70* (Dublin, 1978). The problem arose from the fact that the mediaeval Reformation parish graveyards which fell into the possession of the Church of Ireland at the Reformation had continued to be used for Catholic as well as Protestant burials (incidentally involving the payment by Catholics of burial fees to the Protestant owners); to the growing number of Evangelical zealots within the Church of Ireland this state of affairs amounted to collusion in idolatry. O'Ferrall, *Catholic Emancipation*, p. 49. The dispute led to the opening of new cemeteries at Glasnevin and Goldenbridge. See also Keenan, *Ireland 1800–1850*, pp. 143–5.

26 The activities financed by the Catholic Rent are discussed in O'Ferrall, *Catholic Emancipation*, pp. 58–78.

27 The original has 'Birc'. John Bric, barrister and prominent Catholic Association activist, killed in a duel, 1826.

28 (1803–75) French nationalist/republican historian; a nondenominational Christian who believed the elimination of clerical influence from public life was a prerequisite of progress. He was dismissed from his teaching post in the College de France in 1846 after delivering anti-clerical lectures, collected in books on *The Jesuits* (1843) and *Ultramontanism* (1844).

29 Taylor's account is somewhat compressed. Stuart had been cultivating the seat since late 1824 with the assistance of the Catholic Association, rather than appearing from nowhere at the last minute (as Alexander Dawson did in Louth). In October 1825 he actually had a majority of registered voters 'according to the old system', but by spring 1826 the Beresfords had pulled back by a registration drive among their supporters' tenants – hence the Beresfords' confidence and the risky decision to appeal to the tenants over the head of their landlords (O'Ferrall, *Catholic Emancipation*, pp. 121–33).

30 O'Ferrall *Catholic Emancipation*, pp. 136–40. Lord Oriel was John Foster, last Speaker of the Irish House of Commons and veteran anti-Emancipationist; his candidate was his nephew John Leslie Foster. The leading Orangeman and Evangelical Lord Roden, whose estates were located in South Down and around Dundalk, was represented by Matthew Fortescue. Foster beat Fortescue by five votes, but the Oriel influence was so severely weakened that he retired at the next general election (O'Ferrall, *Catholic Emancipation*, pp. 136–40).

31 Stewart J. Brown, 'The new reformation movement in the Church of Ireland, 1801-29' in Stewart J. Brown and David W. Miller (eds), *Piety and Power in Ireland: Essays in Honour of Emmet Larkin* (Belfast/Notre Dame, 2000), pp. 180–208.

32 Peel's admission to this effect during the Emancipation debates had been revived by the Protectionists in 1846 to accuse Peel of hypocrisy in refusing to serve under the pro-Emancipationist Canning in 1827. Peter Jupp, *British Politics on the Eve of Reform: The Duke of Wellington's Administration, 1829–30* (London, 1998), p. 205.

33 For the context of this statement (10 June 1828) see Jupp, *British Politics on the Eve of Reform*, p. 56.

34 Taylor's account, presented as an eyewitness report by the fictitious 'Munster Farmer' appears to be based on Sheil's recollections of the Clare election, reproduced in M. W. Savage (ed.), Richard Lalor Sheil, *Sketches, Legal and Political* (London, 1855).

35 J. Roderick O'Flanagan, *The Bar Life of O'Connell* (London, 1875); Pronsias O Duigeanain, *The Priest and the Protestant Woman: The Trial of Rev. Thomas Maguire, P.P., December 1827* (Dublin, 1997).

36 'Caffey' in original; Sheil has 'Coffey'.

37 Father of William Smith O'Brien.

38 A bloodthirsty and demented seventeenth-century Presbyterian fanatic in Scott's novel *Old Mortality*. Taylor is echoing Sheil's description of Fr. Murphy of Corofin as resembling Ephraim Macbriar, another zealot in the same novel. Elsewhere in Taylor's writings he loves to emphasise resemblances in manners and methods between Catholic and Protestant zealots.

39 Fitzgerald's supporters later claimed that this incident had been staged; a coffin supposedly containing the voter's remains was paraded through Ennis on the fourth day of polling. The priest was a Fr. Geoghegan. (O'Ferrall, *Catholic Emancipation*, pp. 197–8).

40 Peel's brother-in-law, MP for Derry City and secretary to the Treasury. O'Ferrall *Catholic Emancipation*, pp. 204–5; for an Orange view see R. M. Sibbett, *Orangeism in Ireland and throughout the Empire* (London, n.d. [1938?]), II, pp. 4–5.

41 The Duke of Leinster had been an Emancipationist; the meeting was organised by the prominent Protestant solicitor and landowner Pierce Mahony, who had been closely associated with O'Connell in the Emancipation campaign.

42 Taylor's review of the classic account of the Doneraile trial in *Ireland and its Rulers since 1829* by Daniel Owen Maddyn is in *Athenaeum*, 28 Oct. 1843, pp. 960–2. O'Connell's hostility to Doherty (a Canningite moderate Tory who had supported Emancipation) was intensified by the acquittal of policemen who had fired into crowds at Borrisokane, County Tipperary, causing several deaths. See also Keenan, *Ireland 1800–1850*, pp. 207–11.

43 O'Connell regularly spoke of giving up Repeal if 'justice for Ireland' (a conveniently elastic concept) could be secured under the Union; Taylor converts this tacit invitation to negotiate into a solemn commitment reneged on by O'Connell.

44 O'Connell argued that the increased population of Ireland since the Union entitled her to a commensurate increase in representation.

45 John Matthew Galwey, MP for Waterford, 1832–5.

46 In France the Jesuits were associated with ultramontanism and demands for Church control of education, whereas their Gallican rivals among the secular clergy were prepared to compromise on education with the liberal monarchy of Louis Philippe. (Taylor's apologia for the National Schools mockingly notes the resemblance between the denunciations of mixed education by the Church of Ireland's Church Education Society and the pronouncements on the same subject of Montalembert, a prominent French Liberal Catholic and admirer of O'Connell.) Sir Robert Inglis, a leading Evangelical banker and member of the 'Clapham Sect', coined the description 'Godless Colleges'; he was a hard-line opponent of Catholic Emancipation. When Peel resigned his Oxford University seat in 1828 to seek a mandate for his change of policy on Catholic

Emancipation, Inglis successfully opposed him in the by-election; he believed the Duke of Wellington should have responded to the Clare Election by crushing Ireland with an army commanded by the Duke of Cumberland, Orange Grand Master.

47 The 'Munster Farmer' is presented as having only a vague and distant knowledge of O'Connor's career as leader of the Chartist movement. Taylor was fiercely hostile to O'Connor and the Chartists.

48 Maurice Fitzgerald, knight of Kerry, though a Conservative had supported Emancipation.

49 'Mr. Ghee' in original. R. J. McGhee and the brothers Mortimer and Samuel O'Sullivan were prominent Church of Ireland Evangelical clerics.

50 The implication is that the statement was made by Whately to Taylor himself. In Taylor, *Visit to the Model Schools*, p. 76 a similar statement is attributed to 'a Conservative friend'.

51 The Earls of Enniskillen whose seat was at Florencecourt in South Fermanagh; the third earl was prominent in the Orange Order.

52 Gerald Fitzgibbon had complained about the manner in which Attorney-General T.B. C. Smith conducted the prosecution – J. G. Swift MacNeill, *What I Have Seen and Heard* (London, 1925).

53 O'Connell's leading defence counsel was James Whiteside (a leading Irish conservative, subsequently a law officer and judge), well known for his eloquence.

54 The '82 Club, whose uniform was modelled on those of the 1782 Volunteers as a sign of martial pretensions; the cap was based on that worn by hussars. O'Connell accepted the presidency of the Club to contain it. Richard Davis, *The Young Ireland Movement* (Dublin, 1987).

55 O'Connell was MP for Cork; Thomas Wyse was MP for Waterford.

56 Taylor uses this image in *History of the Civil Wars*, II, p. 166 to describe the difficulty experienced by the Williamite commanders in controlling Enniskillener Protestant irregulars.

57 In August 1839 O'Connell privately spoke of retiring from public life to end his days living among the Jesuit community at Clongowes (MacDonagh, *O'Connell*, p. 463).

58 This lasted a week and took place in 1838. O'Connell helped to arrange the migration of the Cistercian monks to the new abbey in County Waterford after their expulsion from France; the restrictions imposed on French religious orders by the Orleanist monarchy led O'Connell to abandon his initial support for that regime and favour the restoration of the Bourbons.

APPENDIX I

1 William Carleton (1794–1869), son of a smallholder from Prillisk, County Tyrone, novelist and short-story writer renowned for his depiction of pre-Famine peasant life and his exuberant explorations of language. Taylor also reviewed Carleton's *The Fawn of Spring-Vale and other Tales* (*Athenaeum*, 15 May 1841 pp. 385–6) and his novels *Valentine*

M'Clutchy (11 Jan. 1845, pp. 38–9), *Rody the Rover* (14 Feb. 1846, pp. 167–8), *Parra Sastha, or Paddy-go-Easy* (4 July 1846, pp. 679–80). Although critical of some political and religious implications of Carleton's 1830s fiction (written after his conversion to Protestantism and under the influence of the Evangelical Tory Rev. Caesar Otway), Taylor shared the modern view that it was superior as literature to his later work.

2   William Parsons (1800–67), third earl of Rosse; heavily involved in relief work and law enforcement during the Famine, but best remembered for his interest in astronomy, which led him to construct the world's largest telescope in Parsonstown (Birr, County Offaly).

3   The Zoroastrian religion sees the world as shaped by conflict between two deities, the evil Angra Mainya (Ahriman) and the benevolent Ahura Mazda (Ormuzd). Ahriman is expected to reign for 9,000 years before his final defeat.

APPENDIX II

1   Thomas, second baron Ffrench, one of 34 JPs arbitrarily removed from the magistracy (23 May 1843) by Lord Chancellor Sugden as punishment for their activity in the Repeal Association. See James H. Murphy, *Abject Loyalty: Nationalism and Monarchy in Ireland During the Reign of Queen Victoria* (Cork, 2001), pp. 38–40.

2   Frederick Shaw, MP for Trinity College and leader of the Irish Conservative MPs; Robert Jocelyn, third Earl of Roden, the most prominent Orange leader.

3   James Bernard, second Earl of Bandon. The West Cork town of Bandon had a relatively large Protestant population (dating back to the Munster Plantation) and was regarded as a stronghold of Orangeism. O'Connell addressed a monster meeting there on 9 December 1839.

4   This appears to be based on Eoghan Ruadh Ó Suilleabhain's English-language ballad, 'Rodney's Glory'.

5   Taylor initially advanced this theory of Irish Yorkism in *History of the Civil Wars*.

6   Waterloo.

7   O'Connell's Dublin residence.

8   Sarsfield.

9   John O'Hagan (1832–90) who wrote as 'Sliabh Cuilinn'. The ballad is the ultimate source of the nationalist slogan 'ourselves alone', later rendered as 'sinn féin'.

10   John Kells Ingram (1823–1907).

11   Thomas Davis (1814–45).

12   Davis wrote under the pseudonym 'Celt'; his authorship was not made public until after his death. Alcaeus (620–580 BC) Greek lyric poet renowned for love songs (though he also wrote on political matters). Tyrtaeus (*c*.650 BC) wrote martial poetry to spur his fellow-Spartans to heroism in battle.

13   Fr C. P. Meehan (1812–90), romantic historian and Young Ireland activist.